The Language
of Leadership

Communicating for Results

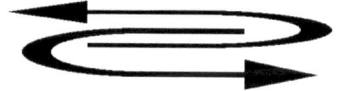

Larry W. Dennis, Sr.

The Language of Leadership
Communicating for Results
Larry W. Dennis, Sr.

Rising Tide Publishing

The Language of Leadership

First Printing 2010

Second Printing 2017

Third Printing 2022

Rising Tide Publishing
Email: larry@turbols.com

ISBN 0-9631766-8-4

Library of Congress No.   2009913503

Cover Design: Richard Ferguson

Editor, Design, Typographics: Esther Hopper

Assistant Editor: Chris Tipp

Manufactured in the U.S.A.

Other books by Larry W. Dennis, Sr.
Life Sentences
15 Principles of Engaging Leadership
How to Turbo Charge You
Repeat Business
InFormation
Making Moments Matter
The Great Baseball Cap
Motorcycle Meditations
15 Leadership Principles & Ronald Reagan

THE LANGUAGE OF LEADERSHIP

TABLE OF CONTENTS

THE LANGUAGE OF LEADERSHIP

COMMUNICATING FOR RESULTS

THE LANGUAGE OF LEADERSHIP is designed to help you dramatically improve your communication skills to maximize your effectiveness as a leader. Effective communication overcomes the greatest challenge in all business and personal relationships.

This book is all about you and how you communicate. You will find meaningful guidance to help you increase the effectiveness of your communication. Use the principles in this book to make a positive difference by:

- ➢ defining the role of communication
- ➢ understanding and overcoming barriers to communication
- ➢ selling your ideas to motivate your listeners
- ➢ ensuring your message has the greatest impact
- ➢ gaining confident competence in speaking before groups
- ➢ conducting better, shorter meetings

You will create the positive actions required to carry out your management objectives. You will strengthen your leadership skills by:

➢ asking pertinent questions
➢ listening for understanding
➢ providing acknowledgment that builds confidence and improves morale
➢ coaching for peak performance
➢ correction for accountability
➢ on-the-job training for empowerment

AND... You will discover a whole new dimension of positive feedback to ensure focus and continued improved performance. In the language of today's leadership, the cutting edge of forward-thinking management technology, Turbo Leadership Systems introduces:

↳*Feedforward/*Feedback↺™.

Learn more in the chapters that follow.

⇤⇥

Introduction

YOU AND COMMUNICATION

THE ABILITY TO COMMUNICATE

As I write this opening to THE LANGUAGE OF LEADERSHIP, the press is full of debate about who will be candidates for the upcoming 2008 presidential campaign. Barack Obama is currently one of the front-runners for the Democratic nomination. Who had even heard of this senator from Illinois three years ago? The answer: Very few. Why is he a front-runner for the Democratic nomination today? His ability to communicate in an inspiring, motivational way created his opportunity: at the Democratic National Convention in 2004, he gave a stirring keynote speech that lasted approximately 30 minutes.

Ronald Reagan, while governor of California, gave an address which immediately gained the attention of the party faithful at the Republican National Convention in 1976. Four years later, at age 69, he was nominated and ultimately elected president of the United States, due in large part to his ability to communicate in a credible, stirring and inspiring way.

Although you are not running for president of the United States, to succeed as a leader you must gain the support of others essential to the success of your enterprise and secure the engagement of your team. You secure this engagement with capable communication. You, like most, have probably not given deliberate attention to the development of communication skills. Up to 90% of your training has been in the technical disciplines of your area of specialty. Still, 80% of your success as a leader depends on your ability to communicate, and win the hearts of your team.

> *You can have brilliant ideas, but if you can't get them across, your ideas won't get you anywhere.*
> — Lee Iacocca

Your ability to communicate, influence, and persuade others to act is absolutely indispensable to everything you accomplish. Empowering leaders communicate in a way that organizes cooperation and energizes support toward the accomplishment of important performance objectives.

THE LIFEBLOOD OF LEADERSHIP

We hear "communication is the secret," or "leadership is communication," and any number of catch phrases about the importance of communication. These expressions are common because they're true.

Think of it this way: Your mission, vision and values are the heart of your organization. Your business plan, systems, and processes are the brain; the various departments and disciplines are its limbs. The lifeblood that activates and motivates the whole enterprise is communication. Communication can be as tactical as assigning tasks, reviewing the daily numbers, listening to associates' input, or as empowering as sharing the purpose and declaring the vision of your organization.

Planning, analyzing, organizing and decision-making are part of your job. Many tasks take up your time. As an empowering leader, your most important role is not merely dealing with these management responsibilities. The most important part of your leadership role is communication, and the purpose of your communication is to get action that leads to desired results.

COMMUNICATING REQUIRES:

- ↳ The ability to make your ideas clear
- ↳ Understanding the nature of the person with whom you are communicating
- ↳ Understanding that communication is an essential part of everything you do
- ↳ Awareness that communication is judged in the context of traditions and practices
- ↳ Understanding that good communication thrives in a climate of trust and confidence
- ↳ Skill in leading meetings
- ↳ A context of understood mission, vision, and values

Too often, the message received is not the message we intend. The communication is filled with so much "static" that the message is not understood or

> *We know communication is a problem, but the company is not going to discuss it.*
> —Plant Supervisor

supported. What causes the lack of clarity that results in communication breakdown? THE LANGUAGE OF LEADERSHIP will help you discover the answers to this question and provide solutions.

⇥

THE GREATEST FRUSTRATION

What is the greatest frustration for most employees? Could it be they think they're not getting paid enough? Or that their workplace is cramped or noisy? Shortage of supplies? Outdated equipment or computers? Inadequate training? Maybe they think management expects too much from them? Could organizational bureaucracy and outdated policies be #1 on their frustration list? These possibilities are easy to imagine—and justify. However, in survey after survey, employees continue to place *communication problems* at the top of their frustration list.

Communication Problems?

Yes, communication problems. Most managers think they spend so much time and effort communicating, it's hard for them to believe communication could be a major problem. The paradox is that while employees are frustrated by a lack of meaningful communication, their managers perceive themselves as outstanding communicators. In a recent study, a group of managers were asked to evaluate their personal communication skills. The study showed that 90% rated their own communication skills in

> ⧽ *Sixty percent of all management problems result from faulty communication.* ⧼ – Peter Drucker

the top 10%. Obviously, 80% of these managers think they are better at communicating than they actually are.

⇥

"Mis-Communication"

Your employees depend on you for the information they need to move in the right direction, to make the right decisions. THE LANGUAGE OF LEADERSHIP will help you acquire the skills to communicate that information to your associates. You will see how to express your ideas in a clear, concise, convincing manner, and ensure the results you want.

Unless you effectively communicate with associates, all your attempts to lead are fruitless. We talk about communication all the time. We seldom share a common definition of communication. You might say our communication about communication breaks down around communication. Here is a humorous but telling example of how communication can go awry:

> **Colonel to his Executive Officer**: "Tomorrow evening at approximately 2000 hours, Haley's Comet will be visible in this area—an event which occurs only once every 75 years. Have the men fall out in the battalion area in fatigues, and I will explain this rare phenomenon to them. In case of rain, we will not be able to see anything, so assemble the men in the theater and I will show them films on it."
>
> **Executive Officer to Company Commander**: "By order of the colonel, tomorrow at 2000 hours, Haley's Comet will appear above the battalion area. If it rains, fall the men out in fatigues. Then march to the theater where the rare phenomenon will take

place—something which occurs only once every 75 years."

Company Commander to Lieutenant*: "By order of the colonel in fatigues, at 2000 hours tomorrow evening, the phenomenal Haley's Comet will appear in the theater. In case of rain in the battalion area, the colonel will give another order—something which occurs once every 75 years."*

Lieutenant to Sergeant*: "Tomorrow at 2000 hours, the colonel will appear in the theater with Haley's Comets—something which happens every 75 years. If it rains, the colonel will order the comet into the battalion area."*

Sergeant to troops*: 'When it rains tomorrow at 2000 hours, the phenomenal 75-year-old General Haley, accompanied by the colonel, will drive his Comet through the battalion area theater in fatigues."*

At that point ... no further comment!

"I Don't Believe We've Met"

It had been a long, revealing and ultimately empowering day with the senior managers of a paper mill in northern British Columbia. It's not easy to look at feedback from peers and employees that conflicts with your view of yourself. After the session ended, we relaxed at the one sports bar in the small mill town. We talked about the day and what they'd learned, and how we could continue to support them in their plans for creating breakthroughs in performance at the mill.

One of the mill's machine oilers was enjoying a game of pool at the other side of the room. He came over to our table with a cue stick in his hand and greeted my partner Ric: "What are you guys doing here?" It was pretty obvious he had consumed several adult beverages.

Ric, who seemed to know him well, told the oiler a little about our day's training. "Well, you know…" the worker confided, "I'm on my two days off. I've been thinking about how we could make the paper winder work better."

Then, turning to me, he said, "I remember you. You're the guy that did that Employee Opinion Survey about a month ago."

"Yes, I am."

"Well, that was pretty important for me. It was really interesting and I appreciated the chance to give my opinions. I hope something comes of it."

Next, the oiler looked over at the plant manager on my right, and said, "I don't think I know you. I don't believe we've met." The plant manager extended his hand and told the man his name.

"Oh!" The slightly inebriated worker, now realizing that this was his plant manager, said, "Good to meet you. Come on down to my area some time."

This same plant manager showed me the questionnaire he used to interview all his senior staff about a year earlier. He had not only interviewed his direct reports; he had categorized and organized their responses into a Pareto chart. His interviews revealed that the greatest "opportunity for improvement" was *communication*.

The bad news is that the plant manager didn't get the point; he didn't realize the importance of connecting with the employees on the floor, who are just as essential to the success of his operation as key staff. Now, a year had passed, and an oiler who cared enough about his work to problem-solve on his days off still had never met his plant manager in person.

The good news? It's never too late to improve communication. Earlier that same day, the manager had committed to pay a visit to every area in the mill.

Within a week he had shown up in person in every department. His "Shoe-Leather Leadership" (see Chapter Nine) continues to this day.

ᴵ⇆ᴵ

COMMUNICATING IN THE "REAL WORLD"

Over the past 24 years, Turbo Leadership Systems has worked with thousands of managers at every level in "hands-on" leadership development programs. The insights gained guide us in the continuous improvement of our programs; the success of organizations across North America and abroad is evidence of the effectiveness of Turbo's approach.

The LANGUAGE OF LEADERSHIP draws on real-life experiences of front-line supervisors, department heads and executive team members. Nothing could be more credible than their real-world stories demonstrating how they put these ideas to the test in the daily challenges of leadership.

"Turbo Terms" - Some "Turbo terms" you'll find in the chapters that follow include:

- ↻ **The Cultural Benchmark Survey™** This initial assessment process highlights the strengths of an organization and pinpoints areas that could be improved.

- ↻ **The 15 Leadership Principles™** form the foundational framework for everything we do. Throughout THE LANGUAGE OF LEADERSHIP are stories of how leaders have used these principles to increase effectiveness.

- ↻ **The "Person Pearl"™** Managers are coached in applying the 15 Leadership Principles with their chosen "Person Pearl." The thread of the "Person Pearl" runs through many of the true-life stories you will read.

- ↻ **5X More Enthusiasm™** Lab members report amazing results when they focus five times (5X) more concentrated laser energy on a project.

- ↻ ⌐*Feedforward*/**Feedback**↻™ You will also learn a totally new definition of feedback and its proper role in creating a *feedforward* organization. You will see how, when properly used, ⌐*feedforward*/feedback↻ literally turbo-charges the performance of your team.

⇋

INTRODUCING... ⌐*FEEDFORWARD*/FEEDBACK↻™

Here's a breakthrough perspective that can revolutionize all your communication:

⌐*Feedforward*/**feedback**↻ is reflective response to your team's performance. It communicates what's needed to achieve excellence and continued improvement.

⌐*Feedforward*/**feedback**↻ clarifies and reinforces performance expectations to ensure your team continually improves. ↳*Feedforward*/feedback↩ is designed to reassure, encourage, support and redirect performance.

The "80/20 formula" applies here: 80% of an empowering leader's ↳*feedforward*/feedback↩ is supportive, while less than 20% is corrective.

Your helpful, supportive ↳*feedforward*/feedback↩ is far more valuable to a high performance team than correction and reprimand.

> ☑ **"I receive the feedback I need to know when I'm doing my job well."**
> –*Cultural Benchmark Survey*

What's Missing Here?

Too often, associates don't get enough ↳*feedforward*/feedback↩ from their manager to know how well they are doing. Without ↳*feedforward*/feedback↩, the team member is left to wonder, "Am I doing OK? Do I need to do something differently?" This uncertainty can affect job performance and diminish job satisfaction.

I recently interviewed all the key employees of a tract-home building construction company. This is a great company. The owners are generous. A liberal bonus system—loans to buy houses, exotic cruises and other tangible benefits—has not created the return they hoped for. The owners are a little frustrated with team members' lack of response to their generosity.

After completing the interviews, I summarized the themes. "Uncertainty" was the predominant theme: associates were not sure whether they were doing the right thing; whether their contribution level was high enough, or valued and appreciated by the owners. One site manager said, "I guess I am doing OK. I have never heard any complaints about my projects."

What the associates need, and have not received, is more ↳*feedforward*/feedback↩; more specific, regular, consistent communication about their job performance.

⇆

THE LANGUAGE OF LEADERSHIP

Empowering leaders see ↳*feed-forward*/feedback↩ as a two-way exchange of communication, the interaction with associates that brings about positive improvements in direction, performance and morale.

> ⋝ *For every action, there is an equal and opposite reaction⋜*

Hiring Interview. ↳*Feedforward*/feedback↩ begins the day a candidate is interviewed and hired. You would not hire them if you didn't feel they were right for the team. They are the best of all the candidates you considered. Too often, from that point forward, leaders don't clearly communicate the roles and responsibilities of the new hire. We fail to offer the ↳*feedforward*/feedback↩ they need to know how they are measuring up on their performance, or to provide guidelines for their success.

On the-Job Training. ↳*Feedforward*/feedback↩ teaches associates how to successfully do their job, and says, "We value you enough to invest additional time and money in your training and development." Never underestimate the cultural impact of basic and ongoing job performance training.

Listening. ↳*Feedforward*/feedback↺ demonstrates a cultural standard that values, respects and appreciates the gifts of each team member. As Ralph Waldo Emerson said, "Every man is my superior in that I learn of him." Listening shows you are open to suggestions, comments and questions.

Acknowledgement. ↳*Feedforward*/feedback↺ is supportive; as an empowering leader, you offer acknowledgement by paying attention, giving approval, appreciation and praise. Your acknowledging ↳*feedforward*/feedback↺ is designed to ensure the behaviors you desire and build the confidence of the receiver.

Coaching. ↳*Feedforward*/feedback↺ helps your associates learn how to perform a task more successfully, more effectively, more efficiently, more safely, or more quickly. It says, "I'd like to offer you some additional personal insights to help you do your job more successfully."

Correcting. ↳*Feedforward*/feedback↺, given in a timely and professional manner, earns respect. It makes the point, "Your behavior is not satisfactory. For you to remain on the team, you must comply with agreed-to standards of performance. We all live in a culture of accountability." Correction that feeds forward ends on a positive note that shows your confidence that associates can and will succeed.

↹

Tips to ↳*Feedforward* for Feedback↺

Get to the point

Sometimes we are tempted to make personal feedback complicated. This may be due in part to our tendency to shy away from any real, direct person-to-person communication. We talk about "things" instead of saying what's really on our mind. The shorter and simpler the message, the better the associate will absorb it, increasing the likelihood of the results you want.

↳*Feedforward*/Feedback↺ is:

Useful. Specific rather than general. "You did a good job with that report" isn't as effective as, "Your charts contrasting last year, same period, really helped me see your point. I was watching as you as spoke, and everyone looked very engaged."

"I appreciate your good work" is not as useful as, "Thank you for paying particular attention to the typeface and style. You gave this piece a very professional look."

Effective. Focused on performance, rather than on the person. It is important to refer to what they do, not who you think or imagine they are. It is more useful to say, "You talked so much no one else could get in a word," than "You are a loudmouth." The first statement allows for the possibility of change; the second implies a fixed personality trait. It hurts the receiver.

Empowering. Points to the strength beneath the performance. Choose one quality you want to amplify and describe it specifically: "You show a lot of determination to support the team in creating those charts, with no help from anyone else. Keep it up."

Considerate. The amount of information the receiver can use rather than the amount you would like to give. Overloading people with information reduces their ability to effectively use it. The first interest of empowering considerate ↳*feedforward*/feedback↰ is helping the other person.

Constructive. Shows and tells how to get things done. Often employees are not doing well because they honestly don't know how to approach a task. Find out if the associate has questions and answer them patiently. Often the person who is afraid to ask questions has a performance problem.

Meaningful. Concentrated on behavior the receiver can change, and on positive changes they can handle. You only frustrate and disempower people when you point out shortcomings over which they have no control, or a physical characteristic they can do nothing about.

Requested. Rather than imposed. It is most useful when the receiver asks for help you can give. You can encourage this by simply saying, "I have an idea that might help. May I mention it?"

Thoughtful. Shares information rather than giving advice unless advice is asked for, leaving people free to decide for themselves. Giving advice is telling them what to do, and can lead to a pushback of defensive resistance.

Impacting. Immediate is best —if the person is ready to hear it. Receiving and using ↳*feedforward*/feedback↩ involves many possible emotional reactions. Give your ↳*feedforward*/feedback↩ at the time it can create the most value.

Objective. Related to what is said or done, not why. Guessing at people's motivations or intentions does not contribute to learning or development. Strike a positive note.

⇆

Now It's Your Turn!

↳*Feedforward*/feedback↩ from your managers, co-workers or associates is the best tool you have for improving your own performance.

This past week, I was practicing for a presentation in front of my 40-year old son. He gave me feedback on my pronunciation of "mirror;" he said I pronounced it *"mear"* instead of *"mir-ror."* It seems my Missouri roots were affecting, and no doubt had affected for over 60 years, my pronunciation of this word, but I didn't know it. I was glad for the feedback.

And few months ago, John, an associate from Cleveland, after watching me teach a Leadership Lab session in Pine Falls, Manitoba, said, "You have a lot to say and are so familiar with your material that sometimes you go so fast I can't keep up with you."

His helpful remark was the reminder I needed to slow down. Even on a tightly timed agenda, I must remember that being

> *Men who know themselves are no longer fools. They stand on the threshold of the door of Wisdom.* –Henry Ellis

understood is more important than staying on schedule.

Encourage others to keep communication open and honest. A study of interpersonal communication using a model called the Johari Window brought out some interesting observations about the blind spots in our behaviors. "People may unwittingly hurt others by giving critical feedback, which is best offered when the receiver is tuned to receive it," the study states. "There are things about ourselves we may not know, but others can see clearly. When others say what they see (feedback) in a supportive, responsible way, and we are able to hear it, we grow and experience more of our true potential."

Here's how to convey that you're open to input:

- ↻ Remember, giving feedback is taking a risk. It's like walking through a minefield. Thank those who are willing to take that risk. Be aware that your response could unintentionally send the message that their comments are unwelcome.

- ↻ Presume they want to help. People who offer feedback are most likely doing so because they want to improve their relationship with you. Those who just want to gripe rarely tell you face to face what they're thinking.

- ↻ Acknowledge their "take" as accurate—from their perspective. Perception is reality. If others say your actions have a negative effect on them, that's the truth for them, regardless of what you intended.

○ Think now, act later. Hearing about our shortcomings almost always hits a nerve, so distance yourself while you decide how to respond.

↹

ACKNOWLEDGING ACKNOWLEDGEMENT

When comments are complimentary, accept graciously. If appropriate, ask how you can continue to improve. Most of us know that the most appropriate response to a compliment is simply "thank you." Yet we make the mistake of throwing the compliment back, trying to disqualify ourselves: "I'm not that good," or "You're just saying that." An appropriate response to a compliment is "Thank you so much! With this in mind, I'm going to continue to . . . "

Receiving an award or a gift is a compliment in a tangible form. The formula for accepting an award is also good for accepting a compliment. Your first words are "thank you." Very often you can then give credit to others: "Thank you very much; I couldn't have done it without my team;" "I couldn't have done it without your help;" "I wouldn't have been able to accomplish this if others hadn't helped." Next, tell how you're going to use the award: "I'll put it on my desk;" "I'll hang it in a prominent place in my office;" "I'll wear it . . . ., and when I do, I'll think of you." Finally, "Thank you again."

Saying Thanks

Many years ago I attended a Wednesday morning professional TIPS club meeting (a group which meets weekly to share business leads). There were more than 30 enthusiastic participants eagerly sharing leads with one another, as they sang the prowess of their own products and services.

I was able to share a lead, which was fun, since it was my first time with the group. I was there as a guest that morning. It always feels good to give. Two or three people who had known me from former affiliations approached me afterward. They wanted to make me feel welcome, and they talked with me about other business opportunities and issues.

Within 24 hours of this meeting, I received a phone call from one of the attendees, and within 48 hours, I'd encountered still another attendee at a second breakfast meeting. And then Friday morning, the president of the club, Carolyn, called to thank me for my attendance and asked if I felt the club was a good fit. I appreciated her call and we had a cordial conversation.

Toward the end of the conversation, I mentioned to her that the noise in the other part of the restaurant had been distracting to me. Carolyn immediately thanked me for bringing the problem to her attention, saying she had not even noticed the distracting noise. I had been a little tentative in mentioning my discomfort—after all, I had been a guest; her club had paid for my breakfast. When Carolyn said she hadn't even noticed it, I was glad I mentioned it. And when she said, "Thank you for bringing it to my attention," I was even happier that I had taken a little risk, a little exercise of courage.

The lesson I learned from this experience is the importance

of bringing to people's attention things they do, or don't do, that may affect me negatively. I experienced firsthand the importance of accepting all feedback in an open, non-defensive manner—the way Carolyn responded with her friendly, grateful 'thank you for bringing this to my attention' response.

The Breakfast of Champions

When you think about it, feedback is the breakfast of champions. Hopefully, you will continue to receive feedback, which will enable you in turn to feed forward to further improve your performance. This will keep you on your own personal path of continuous improvement.

Chapter One

What Is Communication?

The Greatest Invention

While watching the Discovery Channel, I was intrigued by a program on great inventions, beginning with the invention of the wheel. The automobile is near the top of my list of great inventions, along with motorcycles, refrigeration, telephones, and airplanes. The invention of the Gutenberg press led to rising literacy and an explosion of knowledge in the early days of the Renaissance. The invention of the cotton gin and harnessing water power gave rise to the Industrial Revolution. And now the invention of personal computers, cell phones, satellites, and the Internet, has birthed the Information Age.

The greatest invention of all time is not any of these wonders. The greatest invention of all time is language. Most of us, from a very early age, acquire language so gradually that we are not aware of how deeply it affects our lives.

Helen Keller lost her sight and hearing before she learned to talk. When she began to learn sign language, her world was reshaped in a sudden burst of new perceptions. Language gave her for the first time a sense of the past and the future. She began to experience language as a force that makes us human, that allows us to dream, to plan, to set and realize goals.

Language gives us the ability to express ideas, the ability to transfer our feelings and thoughts. In mastering the use of this invention we experience fulfillment in human relations and effectiveness as leaders. As you strengthen your ability to communicate, you gain a sense of personal power that cannot be obtained in any other way.

↹

GREAT COMMUNICATION

Stop for just a moment and think about some of the influential people in your life, people you respect: coaches, teachers, ministers, managers, coworkers and friends. It's a good bet that the people who had the deepest influence on your life were great communicators. This doesn't necessarily mean they had flawless grammar or an extensive vocabulary, though good grammar and a growing vocabulary are desirable and worth pursuing. Great communication is more. Great communication is delivering your message for the widest possible impact. Great communication is the language of leadership.

There is a kind of intensity, sincerity, urgency, and credibility that punctuates and underlines the words of great communicators. Great communicators are able to penetrate preoccupation, stimulate interest, overcome skepticism, and create desire that motivates us to action. Great communicators capture our minds, ignite our imaginations and win our hearts; they change our thinking, our direction, our conclusions, and ultimately, the quality of our lives.

↹

THE COMMUNICATION LOOP

Communication is a loop; it requires both a capable sender and a receptive receiver. At its best, communication is a deep, honest, respectful two-way interaction between the sender and the receiver. As an empowering leader, you communicate in a way that opens the door for the receiver to respond positively, helping you achieve the desired results.

Communication, at its deepest level, is true understanding. When you break down the word "understanding," you get "under-standing," the foundation you stand on. It goes back to the colloquial expression of "make a stand," or "what you stand for." We all seek to be understood; feeling misunderstood is one of the most frustrating, debilitating and disempowering feelings we ever experience.

At the heart of real communication is a determination to be understood. If your ideas are rejected, you at least want to know that they were understood before being rejected. The feedback you receive is your answer.

Anytime you say, "They didn't understand," you have missed a fundamental of communication: It's your responsibility as the sender to be understood, not the responsibility of the receiver to understand. When you say, "I don't understand," you might mean: "I don't see what you are saying—the message isn't clear."

> *≷It's not their job to understand; it's your job to be so clear that there is no room for misunderstanding. ≷*

Or, you might mean: "I see what you're saying, but I don't agree with your point of view or your conclusion."

The first step to better communication is committing to being responsible for getting the message across. Think through your message:

- ↻ What is my point?
- ↻ Why should they listen?
- ↻ What do I want them to understand?
- ↻ What problem will this solve for them?
- ↻ How will this make their life better?
- ↻ What response do I want?

Boil your message down to its main points. Determine how you can best gain favorable attention. Be specific, with appropriate details. Use examples to penetrate preoccupation and create credibility.

⇆

THE HEART OF LEADERSHIP

Communication skill is at the heart of leadership. Everything we do as leaders requires capable communication. The word "communication" comes from the same source as commu-nity" and "communion." It means to be in relationship. Relationship is when we share the same footing, the same foundation. Poor relationships are caused by *mis*-un-derstandings. Great communication eliminates the root source of communication breakdowns, and ensures understanding.

Your communication style is a habit. Developing new and improved communication skills requires commitment, and the determination to break old patterns. As you improve your communication skills, you are exercising your responsibility to get your ideas across more effectively, more often. Increasing your skill in communicating your ideas and expressing your feelings will streamline your day-to-day effectiveness, and expand your ability to impact the subtle dynamics that govern all human relations.

By definition, management means getting work done through the efforts of others. You may be able to get short-term results by dominating and pressuring your team, but you are not likely to achieve the goals of your organization. To be effective as a manager, you must be sensitive to the needs of the people on your team, the need to be treated with respect, to feel competent and independent. Be sure you are communicating in a way that generates new learning, invites honesty and forthrightness, and builds the mutual trust that is essential to productive working relationships.

> *There's life and death in the power of the tongue.*
> —Proverbs 18:21

THE MEASURE OF EFFECTIVENESS

The effectiveness of your communication is measured by the response you receive. In other words, what you get back defines the message you are sending. The intent of your communication, or simply saying the right words, does not necessarily mean that others understand you and will respond the way you want them to. We all know the frustration of seeing a blank look on the face of the person we're trying to communicate with. Then, what a sense of triumph when their face lights up, and they say, "I see what you mean!"

You have successfully communicated your idea when the picture in your receiver's mind is a match for the picture in your mind, and when the feeling in your receiver's heart matches the feeling in yours. This is real communication.

᛭

Cliff Hanger

Norman, president and owner of a general contracting firm, illustrated this point with his story:

> "One summer several of my friends and I pitched a camp-site at the Cougar Reservoir. Our campsite was located on the dry lake bottom, near the edge of a sharp 12-foot drop-off to the river channel that flowed through the center of the lake bed. Our identifying landmark was a large stump hanging out over the edge of the channel.
> "The night was pitch dark, clouded over—not a star in the sky. We built a great big bonfire and got several people from other campsites together for a visit. Later in the evening, a man from a neighboring camp, unfamiliar with the layout of our site, asked about the location of a 'bathroom.' My friend pointed toward the stump and said, 'A good place to go is over by that stump, just past the light of the campfire.'

"The visiting camper walked out of the bright light of the campfire toward the stump, and stepped off of the edge of the cliff! I will never forget the sound of his screams, nor the chaos that followed in our camp. It took a concerted team effort to get the man back up the cliff to the campsite, and then into our car and off to the hospital as fast as we could. We were all afraid that by the time we got him up and out it might be too late to save him.

"The man's 12-foot fall resulted in head injuries requiring multiple stitches, but no broken bones. We were all relieved he only needed stitches—he could have been killed!

↪*"The lesson I learned from this experience is how important it is to be clear in all my communication. I need to be specific when giving directions. Failing to communicate clearly always results in loss, and can carry a high cost."*

NUMBER ONE

So, where do you begin? What do empowering leaders talk about? Your number one assignment is to communicate the mission, vision, values and goals of your organization. I first helped a client company write a mission statement in 1972. I take pride in having been an early adapter, a pioneer, in this area. Very few companies had clearly defined mission statements in those days. I didn't fully understand the value of establishing and publishing the mission of the organization. I knew it was important, but I didn't know how important. In ensuing years, organizations have become increasingly aware of the necessity to clearly articulate and communicate the animating principles of their mission, vision and values.

Some leaders seem almost embarrassed to talk about their ideals. If talking about purpose is out of your comfort zone, so be it. Talking about the purpose of your organization and department, and your commitment to it, will only become part of your comfort zone by doing it—no matter how nervous, awkward or uncomfortable you may feel. I am not asking, or recommending, that you talk about something you don't believe in. If you don't believe in the mission of your organization, if you don't believe your organization serves some purpose beyond that of making a profit, you have missed the point. Let's remember that profit is how you keep score, how you provide a return on the risk capital of owner-investors. Profit is not the purpose of your organization.

The purpose of your organization is to meet some human need, to provide solutions that solve customers' problems. If you solve customer problems more creatively than others, you get to stay in the game; you have capital for future investments, rewards for your team and dividends for your investors. If you are far better at it than your competitors, you get to make an unusually good return on your investment, which you are certainly entitled to.

᛭

People Need to Believe

Stating the overarching purpose of the organization is just the beginning. It is essential to ensure that all associates understand the importance of their individual part in the achievement of that purpose. Every day, workers leave one organization and go to work for another, not for more money alone, but because of their hope that they can believe more in the purpose and the people in their new organization.

Talk about your mission, vision, values, the purpose of your organization! Your associates want to hear about it; they need to hear about it; they need to believe in it. At the end of the day, they need to know that what they do, matters.

If your purpose is to fulfill customers' needs and societal problems, at a higher level than others, then you have a mission and a right to talk about it! The great news is that as you talk about your purpose, you are meeting the needs of your associates as assuredly as you are meeting your own. Your associates need and want to give their hearts to a worthy cause. It is part of their human makeup, part of their DNA.

If you don't believe that you are in business for anything more than to make money, you will have to buy, with money, the hands of your team members. You cannot, and will never be able to, buy their hearts. Your communication must ensure that all associates have a line of sight from their work to the mission of your organization. This is how you win the hearts of your associates.

↤↦

Are You Being Discounted?

Do you have people in your organization who are more engaged, who work harder, more enthusiastically, in their volunteer activities than in the work they do for you? If so, that's unfortunate. Unfortunate, because your associates are discounting the value of the work they do for you. *You are not getting full value.*

Your associates are delivering discounted value because they don't find meaning in their work; you are receiving discounted value from them because their hearts are not in their job. This is a "lose-lose." When you turn this around and give by communicating purpose, your associates see how they contribute to something worthwhile. You secure their hearts. This is your charge as an empowering leader.

Winning your team's hearts is your job. It may be a tough job. When done successfully, it is a meaningful job, a fulfilling job. The tool you use is the language of leadership— ⌐*feedforward*/feedback ↄ.

↤⌐→ı

EARN TRUST

At the time of the Industrial Revolution, business owners and ship's captains literally held in their hands the fates of their crews and workers. Today, leaders no longer wield such threatening control. You must rely on persuasion, engagement and inspiration to secure the hands, heads and hearts of your team. Often, managers bemoan the challenges and responsibilities that accompany leadership. I seriously doubt they would want to return to those former times. So let's give up wishing for another time and revel in the present, when no one can be forced, out of fear, to do their job.

Today, all engagement is "voluntary." You can't force anyone to do anything; you must be skillful at persuasion. By definition, leadership means getting things done through the efforts of other people.

As an empowering leader, you achieve long-term effectiveness by being sensitive to the needs of those who work for and with you. You may be able to get short-term results by pressuring and dominating associates, but you will not achieve any long-terms goals. It is not healthy or profitable to manipulate people; it is essential to establish a relationship of honesty and trust. When you treat your associates with respect, giving them the opportunity to feel competent and independent, you are creating a team that is highly motivated to achieve their own goals and dedicated to the goals of your organization.

Empowering leaders communicate a climate of trust where associates have permission to experiment and take risks without fear of penalty. Permission and protection include celebrating mistakes and applauding intentions of "playing to win."

To be an empowering leader who has earned the trust of your associates, you must project total credibility. As demonstrated in study after study through the 1960s, '70s, and '80s by Dr. James McCroskey, Dept. of Communication Studies, University of Alabama, and other researchers, there are five qualities necessary for a communicator to be accepted as credible. These five qualities are competence, character, composure, likability, and high energy. In ensuing chapters you'll find a treasury of time-tested ideas and insights to skillfully project your leadership abilities and ensure your credibility.

> *Every time we open our mouth, someone looks inside our mind.*

Empowering means helping associates confidently and competently accept increased responsibility. People either feel that their job is merely to survive and ask for as much as possible in terms of monetary reward, or, they want to thrive and contribute to the overall purpose and vision of the organization. Whether they choose to survive or thrive is a function of whether they are being managed or led. Your choice: your communication with associates can create a climate where you must continually push, cajole, control. Or, you can inspire your team with ↳*feedforward*/feedback↰ that leads to a desire to learn, grow, and create.

↰↲

Genuine Interest Builds Trust

Dani, expediter for a manufacturer, gives it a try:

"In the past few weeks, I have been working closely with Dave, in our shipping department. Dave is relatively new. We didn't have a bad working relationship, but something was missing. We didn't communicate as well as I wanted. Dave's response to my inquiries and suggestions seemed clipped, guarded and restrained. He never initiated any communication with me.

"I decided to *become genuinely interested* in Dave (*Leadership Principle #2*) and see if I could stimulate him to a greater level of self-confidence. I started going out of my way to speak with him about personal and work-related subjects. Before long, Dave started to more fully respond to my comments and inquiries. He started asking me questions and asking for my suggestions. My office is located upstairs and away from the shipping department so it takes a special effort to get up there. Before I knew it,

Dave was going out of his way to come upstairs to see me in my office and speak to me about whatever was on his mind. He actually started by offering suggestions on how to do things differently, to eliminate errors and be more productive. He is now quite willing and able to communicate his ideas openly and freely. The communication between the two of us has become much better, and he is comfortable enough to proactively offer his own suggestions. Problems are eliminated before they arise, and our team performs more successfully.

ᕤ*"The lesson I learned from this experience is that by expressing genuine interest in others, I can actually raise their confidence, and help create an environment that encourages others to take the risks required for us to operate as an innovative team."*

ᕀᕀ

RAPPORT

To be successful as a proactive communicator, you begin by establishing rapport.

> ⸮ *Rapport is like money; it increases in importance when you don't have it, and when you do have it, many opportunities appear.* ⸮

Rapport is a somewhat exotic English word derived from the French verb *rapporter*, meaning to bring back or refer. The English meaning, *a relation of harmony, conformity, accord, or affinity*, indicates the importance of rapport in communication. It is a most important ingredient in any interaction. Without rapport, you will not get what you want—improved relationships, cooperation, and the energetic engagement of your team.

You can intentionally create rapport when you sense it is missing. How? Actually, you do it often! The following will help you remember:

Seven Ways to Create "RAPPORT"

> **R... Remember names**—get committed to learning and using people's names. This starts with really listening for their name when you first hear it.

> **A... Attitude**—display a positive attitude—smile if you feel good inside. If you don't, smile anyway; you'll feel better. People will reflect your smile back to you. You always like a person who makes you smile.

> **P... People**—stop looking for interesting people—start showing interest in people (Leadership Principle #2: *Become Genuinely Interested*).

> **P... Personal mannerisms**—match the other person's style. Mirror their tone of voice, their rhythm and speed of speaking, their breathing rate, their physical position and posture.

> **O... Open your mind**—be receptive to your listeners. Develop a healthy curiosity and inquiring mind. (See Chapter Two, Asking the Right Questions.)

> **R... Recognize**—good qualities, traits and behaviors in people and tell them what you see! (Leadership Principle #4: *Provide Acknowledgement*) See Chapter Nine, Acknowledgment.

> **T... Talk**—encourage the other person to talk—and let them to do most of the talking! (Leadership Principle #6: *Be an Active Listener*) See Chapter 8, Listening.

The most effective tool you can employ is the gift of your active attention, listening, without criticism, to what the associate has to say. Your associates will take actions on suggestions only when they know they can trust the person who is making them. Increasing your understanding of others and your skills for communicating effectively will help you create more positive, responsive, productive relationships with your team.

⇄

SUMMARY

Actions for Empowering Leaders:

- ↺ Commit to improving your communication practices
- ↺ Communicate your mission, vision and values
- ↺ Take full responsibility for being understood
- ↺ Measure communication effectiveness by the responses
- ↺ Establish rapport by expressing genuine interest

The Benefits You Will Gain

- ↺ You will have improved relationships
- ↺ You will connect with your team
- ↺ Your ideas will be put into action
- ↺ You will feel empowered
- ↺ Morale and motivation will improve

Chapter Two

BARRIERS TO COMMUNICATION

Barrier: anything that obstructs, restrains or separates

A FAILURE TO COMMUNICATE

When the Captain said to Cool Hand Luke, "What we have here is a failure to communicate," he was not talking about a lack of information. He was referring to Cool Hand Luke's apparent lack of understanding about the seriousness of the situation. Do you ever see breakdowns in communication on your team, in your department, or between you and other important people in your life? Could you say, "What we've got here is a failure to communicate?" Lack of effective communication is, indeed, the number-one management problem.

We all, at our core, want understanding and communication. Why is communicating so tough?

Communication breaks down for one or more reasons:

- ➢ The inability to effectively express ideas
- ➢ Failing to see the importance of sharing information
- ➢ A reluctance to courageously express ideas

Individual Differences Create Barriers

You do not communicate in a vacuum. People you communicate with have their own traditions, cultural norms—biases, vested interests, points of view, fears and previous experiences. These biases and preconceived notions add to your challenge in being understood.

No two people are completely alike. We all have differing opinions, attitudes, beliefs, values, work habits, goals, ambitions, and dreams. Because of this rich diversity, it has never been more difficult for leaders to form their people into a closely aligned team.

Often, the mistakes we make in communicating are caused by our failure to consider individual differences in the makeup of people. Differences contribute to barriers, and barriers create a filter between you and your listener. Some of the potential barriers include:

1. Temperaments
2. Assumptions
3. Viewpoints
4. Attitudes
5. Values

⇆

BARRIER #1: TEMPERAMENT

Temperament: the combination of an individual's mental and emotional traits

Varying degrees of assertiveness, security, structure and creativity combine to form individual temperaments. Be aware of what "pushes your buttons." Your temperament naturally affects the way you communicate, and is reflected in your tone of voice, word choice and body language.

As an empowering leader, you understand that team members' reaction to your feedback is greatly impacted by their individual temperaments. You respect and consider their differences and tailor your communication accordingly, continuing to lead from a position of strength.

⇆

There are two general types of temperament:

Dominant and Supportive

Dominant: The person with a dominant temperament is assertive, strong-willed and often the first to speak up. Dominant individuals want to control their environments. They have a strong sense of purpose, and see obstacles as mere challenges. They are oriented to look at the final results, and move quickly to action. They sometimes appear insensitive and blunt. They may be seen by others as impetuous and impulsive—wanting action merely for the sake of action. Dominant personalities may be defined as:

- Independent—single-minded and determined to win
- Competitive—plays to win at all costs
- Assertive—outspoken, tries to dominate others
- Spontaneous—flexible and non-traditional
- Innovative—a casual attitude toward rules and traditions

To communicate with a dominant person, you need to be efficient in presenting your case. Lead with clear, concise feedback. Demonstrate support for their ideas, present practical solutions to problems, and provide a few options for them to choose from.

Supportive: Team members with a supportive temperament get the work done. They prefer secure, stable environments and may resist change. You will seldom find them leading an organization; they often shun ultimate responsibility. They need time to get to know you; and you need to take the time to get to know them. Supportive personalities may be described as:

- ↳ Diplomatic—avoids conflict and chooses to encourage others
- ↳ Cooperative—contributes to the work of the team
- ↳ Submissive—takes a diplomatic approach to disagreements
- ↳ Conscientious—likes to work within a set of highly defined, traditions

To lead supportive personalities, rely on plenty of positive ↳*feedforward*/feedback↶.

↹

Jerry Takes the High Road

Jerry, senior project manager for a major general contractor, told how the "Person Pearl" worked for him:

"My boss is my 'Person Pearl.' He is the Vice President of Operations of our firm. He is a very experienced and capable individual. Starting out as a carpenter, he rose through the levels of carpenter foreman and superintendent to operations manager. He is a talented construction specialist.

"He is defined by the Meyers Briggs personality type

indicator as an ISTJ personality type, an 'Introverted Sensing Thinking Judger.' Without going into all of the details, this means that it is not his natural tendency to be a warm, friendly, outgoing people-person. He is inclined to quietly and independently do his job and do it very well.

"I, too, am an ISTJ personality. Following my natural inclination, I was quietly completing projects on time and within budget, but something didn't feel right. I was uncertain of my contribution and effectiveness. This uncertainty led, I now realize, to self-doubt and fear. I received very little feedback—maybe nothing was wrong.

"Some managerial theory says you should meet with a person and ask if there is something wrong. With the confidence provided by the Leadership LAB, I decided instead to take the high road. I confidently told myself that there was nothing wrong. It was just my turn to take positive action.

"When he assigned my projects to other personnel, I jumped on Leadership Principle #8 and 'Validated His Ideas.' I didn't merely accept his personnel assignments; I actively supported them. On those occasions when we did discuss work, my first response was to 'Begin With Yes, Yes, yes' (Leadership Principle #14). I couldn't believe how easy it was.

"My 'Person Pearl' isn't quite ready for harvest. The raise he gave me two weeks ago has reinforced my resolve to take the other person's temperament into consideration, and not overlook the relationship of their perception to my success. Things are getting better all the time. Communication is easier, more open and friendly. The door is now open for the relationship to keep improving.

↳ *"The lesson I learned from this experience is that individual personality differences impact communication. To have successful communication, I must understand and take into consideration, the other person's personality and temperament."*

↹

BARRIER #2: ASSUMPTIONS

Assumption: Something taken for granted; a supposition

What's Wrong with This Picture?

1) ***Employee Assumes*** personal production rate is satisfactory.

    Manager: Called a special meeting and announced, very briskly, "Something has to change around here. Everyone has to get on the ball. If business is not better taken care of, some changes will be made."

    Employee Assumes the manager meant changes in employee's job security.

    Manager Meant a change in systems, processes and methods.

2) **Manager** has not spoken to nor greeted the new employee in the several weeks she has been on the job.

    New Employee Assumes that the manager has no interest in how she is doing; she becomes frustrated.

Manager Assumes the new employee is doing well and enjoying her work because there have been no complaints.

A proactive leader eliminates the need for guesswork by being aware that team members' assumptions affect the way communication is received and understood, and may often lead to misconceptions that impact attitude and performance.

↹

An Assumed Lack of Attention

Nancy, manager for an equipment manufacturer, gives a good example:

"There had been a lot of tension among the manufacturing supervisors concerning the attention the director had been giving to certain supervisors in the manufacturing department. It was felt that in our production meetings, only a few of the supervisors were acknowledged, recognized and verbally rewarded for their efforts and achievements. When the director came out to the production areas, he seemed to spend time only with these favorite people. The other supervisors were starting to feel snubbed. A lack of trust in the director was beginning to develop.

"I had approached the director once before about his appearing to show favoritism towards new supervisors who have college degrees. So I had to drum up the courage to set an appointment with him a second time. When I told him what was being said about him on the floor, he seemed shocked. He said he had been trying to stay away from the new people. Actually, it became evident the problem was that although he was staying away from the new supervisors, he still was not acknowledging the experienced long-term supervisors. The old-timers assumed he was playing favorites.

"As we talked, he began to realize this issue was really a comfort zone problem. He admitted he tended to spend the most time with the supervisors who had reported directly to him in the past, people he had been involved in selecting. He simply felt more comfortable with them. He could see the need to include all his supervisors and spend more time with the whole team. He made a commitment not just to me, but to himself, to spend equal time with all of the supervisors, and asked me to let him know if he didn't follow through on his commitment.

↳*"The lesson I learned from this experience is the importance of staying alert to associates' assumptions that can lead to false conclusions, creating doubt and mistrust."*

⇄

BARRIER #3: VIEWPOINTS

Viewpoint: a particular manner of perceiving, based on personal position, experience or interests

An idea that motivates you to action might be a "turn-off" to someone else. Whether a person acts or chooses not to act on a certain idea depends on their personal viewpoint. If the way *you* see people, things and life is in harmony with the way *they* see them, successful communication is easy. If not, it is difficult to communicate. One of the best steps to successful communication is to "See Things From the Other Person's Point of View "(*Leadership Principle #5.)*

When people from Sales and Accounting meet, they bring their own biases and viewpoint with them. When Production and Distribution get together, they bring their preconceived notions. By understanding another's point of view you can position your communication in terms of the other person's interests. Plan your communication taking their point of view into consideration.

⇆

Eliminate the Negative

Mike, swing shift supervisor for a manufacturer, changes his view:

"I have been the swing shift supervisor of our shop for some time now. Recently, a new day shift supervisor was appointed. I had some built-in, preconceived negative notions about him. After a few brief encounters, I felt that these notions were justified. I found myself getting defensive and taking offense at little things he said. I got to the point where I was focusing all of my energy on avoiding him at shift change so I wouldn't have to see or be forced to talk to him.

"When we were asked to select someone, private or professional, to be our 'Person Pearl,' I thought, what the heck, I need to make my relationship with this guy work, so I picked the day shift supervisor. The very act of writing 'Ed' down on the card, stating my intention, began the process that resulted in my commitment to improving our relationship. The shift had occurred internally.

"I began by being more open-minded and nonjudgmental. I realized that I had never really given Ed a chance to be a decent person in my eyes. I had made my prejudices my reality. When I really started to think about it, I saw Ed as a potential friend. I even noticed a few areas where he and I actually had something in common. I went straight for these areas, and began to develop my friendship with Ed. I feel our relationship has vastly improved.

"Ed didn't realize he was my 'Person Pearl' until a few weeks later, when I decided to share it with him. I now realize that everything that I thought was bad about him was really all in my head. I had let a few incidents justify my negative viewpoint about him, and I put a huge barrier between us. That wedge would have been permanent if I had not done something about it.

⟲ *"The lesson I learned from this experience is to not let my preconceived, negative notions affect my view of someone. I know that it would be almost unnatural to have no preconceived notions. So, if I must have them, I will choose to err on the positive side."*

⇥

BARRIER #4. ATTITUDES

Attitude: manner or disposition that affects the way one interacts with people and situations

Attitudes are our feelings toward life, our response to our world. The most important question you can ask yourself is this: "Is this a friendly universe?" Your answer to this question, whether it's yes or no, defines your attitude toward life. Your response to the cliché, "Is the glass half empty or half full?" reflects your attitude.

Your attitude toward life, your work, your feelings about yourself, and your feelings about others in general, are all potential barriers. If you're a "half full" person and the other is a "half empty," that's a barrier. If you're a "This is a friendly universe" and the other is a "This is a hostile universe," you have a potential barrier. If someone does not approve of your organization and you do, that's a potential barrier. You see yourself as a victor—you somehow always win, you're lucky—and they see themselves as a victim—they are unlucky, they always lose. These closely held attitudes and feelings about life, are inherently barriers to effective communication.

⇄

Don't Wait for the Annual Review

Bob, store manager for a craft and hobby supply company, adjusts an attitude:

"Last Monday, I was talking with Pam, my assistant manager in Beaverton. Our store has been open for almost exactly one year now. I had chosen Pam as my 'Person Pearl,' a person I wanted to improve my relationship with. The main reason I chose Pam is because I realized we have totally different attitudes toward our work. Pam tends to be much more random in her approach, just does what is in front of her. Sometimes she had seemed forgetful, unorganized and haphazard. I'm more linear in my work habits and approach to tasks.

"I mentioned her upcoming bi-yearly review and she half-jokingly said, 'I guess I should start getting worried.' I said, 'Actually, Pam, you should look forward to your review because I've noticed a great deal of personal and professional growth in you this past six months.' I gave her some specific examples of things I had observed and instantly a look of delighted surprise appeared on her face. It was obvious to me she was glad I noticed and acknowledged her efforts and accomplishments!

"I have a natural inclination to jump in and finish the job if I think it's going too slow or not to my liking. I took time to notice Pamela's efforts and better appreciate her style of working.

↳"The lesson I learned from this experience is that I can overcome differences by being alert to my associates' inherent attitudes. I don't need to wait till the annual review to take time to reassure my people. I have learned to trust and appreciate others' styles of working."

BARRIER #5. VALUES

Values: ideals, customs, principles, standards or spiritual qualities of mind and character

Core values are the organizing principles that determine how people live their life. It's the way we live that reflects our values. Values can differ greatly from person to person. Some people place a high value on family, others on independence. Some people value leisure, others hard work. Some place a high value on freedom, others on commitment. Some value spontaneity, others favor planning. Some place a high value on frugality, others on pleasure. Some value serving the customer, and others place a high value on their own needs and desires. Some value physical fitness, others comfort and ease. Some place a high value on adventure and growth, and others on security and safety.

You must understand the values of others if you wish to get in step, and create the rapport and understanding that's required to penetrate communication barriers. My experience in working with management teams convinces me that we have not paid enough attention to the foundational cultural values that stimulate and motivate team members.

⇄

WHAT ARE YOU COMMUNICATING?

To successfully communicate, it's also important for you to understand your own values and how they color the way you show up for your associates. As the leader, you're in the spotlight. You are always being silently critiqued. Take a look for yourself at your leadership style. You could be coming across with:

➢ **Judgment.** When you judge others, you automatically wall yourself off from impartial listening to their ideas. You are discounting their opinions or deciding they're wrong before you've given yourself an opportunity to objectively evaluate what you're hearing.

➢ **Superiority.** Communicating a feeling of superiority in position, power or ability implies that others are inadequate. There tends to be a sense of one-upmanship to this approach.

➢ **Certainty.** Communicating in a manner that implies you know all the answers suggests that there is no need or desire for additional information. You display the need to be right, even to the point of winning an argument rather than solving a problem.

➤ **Control.** When you try to change or restrict the behavior or attitude of others by imposing your set of values on them, you are controlling. A person who engages in this behavior has a high need to run others and every situation.

➤ **Manipulation.** Communicating with hidden motives in a way that uses others to meet your own needs is manipulation. This type of communication has a "gotcha" feeling.

➤ **Indifference.** Showing a lack of interest or concern for the feelings and welfare of the other person implies the other person's views are unimportant.

If you are unconsciously communicating these messages, they may be silently overriding what you want your associates to hear.

↤⇥

Debate or Dialogue?

Think of your communication as a two-way interaction, rather than a debate that attempts to prove you are right. According to professional mediator Mark Gerzon, who has worked as a facilitator and leadership trainer for the United Nations, the US House of Representatives, and a wide range of corporate and civic organizations around the world, people don't want more speeches and presentations; they don't want more debates that skirt difficult issues. What they yearn for is honest, inclusive dialogue that recognizes that people have differing viewpoints, temperaments and attitudes, and creates communication across the barriers that separate them.

A dialogue is designed for situations where people may have fundamentally different mindsets, world views, or belief systems. When you address issues that concern your associates, are you entering into a debate, or are you inviting dialogue, laying a foundation for trust and cooperation?

Check it out:

Debate:	**"There is one right answer—mine."**
Dialogue:	"Maybe a lot of people have pieces of the answer"
Debate:	"It's all about winning."
Dialogue:	"Let's look for common ground."
Debate :	Points out flaws and weaknesses in others' views
Dialogue:	Listens to understand, find meaning and agreement
Debate:	Defends their own views
Dialogue:	Admits others' thinking can improve their own

Focus on Favorable Facets

Diana, assistant station manager for a major truck plaza, gets a new focus:

"Early in March, I started in my new position as the Assistant Station Manager. Within the first few days, most of the employees on my crew had shared with me their dislikes about one particular employee. They said she would flash a big smile at customers and say all the right things. Then she would turn around and make catty, caustic, biting remarks about and toward fellow team members. Her associates believed she was short and impatient with other employees. When they tried to offer her guidance or help, she was often very rude, defensive and completely unreceptive.

"Even though these opinions about her seemed to be universal, I knew I needed to form my own authentic conclusion, not work from hearsay. As I began my own observations, I found that many of their complaints were well-founded. I forced myself to look more closely at this employee, and began to find some important positive qualities.

"When I decided it was time to talk to her, I was thoughtful and direct in my approach. I prepared myself to be ready, willing and eager to listen to her side. As she talked, I realized that her unprofessional behavior was not intentional. I spent some time coaching her in the use of what were, for her, new and different communication skills. When I heard what I believed was a sincere effort on her part to improve communication with one of her associates, I praised her for a job well done. In a short time, others were more willing to share their positive observations of her attainments as she began to display a willingness to receptively listen. Also to my delight, I began to notice other employees changing the way they approached each other to exchange information.

"This was a very delicate, potentially volatile situation that required communicating with conscious, clear intention and sincere interest. The lesson I learned is that the effort required to effectively communicate pays off for the whole team."

What you focus on amplifies and expands. It would have been easy for Diana to be pulled into the pattern of focusing only on the shortcomings, the difficulties, the problem. Instead, she exercised the discipline that was required to see the good in the performance of the challenging employee, to recognize her positive characteristics. As she paid attention to her positive qualities, the positive qualities began to overshadow the negative traits in the entire team, not just in the problem person.

⇌

YOUR "PERSON PEARL"™

Pick a person with whom you feel some friction or distance. Identify some of the things you like about the person, and start focusing on and talking about those things. You may be amazed at the results. Take a few minutes to contemplate the following questions:

- ➤ In what ways is this person similar to me?
- ➤ In what ways is this person different from me?
- ➤ What mistakes have I made in communicating with this person because of these differences?

With this information in mind, what will you begin to do differently to improve the results of your communication with this person?

⇌

SUMMARY

Actions for Empowered Leaders:

- ↻ Think through the background and experience of your listener
- ↻ Be on guard against making quick judgments
- ↻ Be open-minded and tolerant of the other person's style
- ↻ Treat others with respect and dignity
- ↻ Notice how your own temperament affects communication

Benefits You Will Gain:

- ↻ You will have stronger relationships with your associates
- ↻ You will have a self-assured team
- ↻ You will live with less stress
- ↻ You will create a more positive work atmosphere
- ↻ You will eliminate costly misunderstandings

Chapter Three

SELLING YOUR IDEAS

SHIPPING OUT YOUR IDEAS

If my granddad, who was a farmer, woke up with an idea about how to get greater yield from his little farm, all he had to do was go into action—do it. Not so for you and me: if we wake up, as we often do, with an idea about how to improve productivity, sales, customer service, quality, inventory turns or profit, we need the support, encouragement, permission or approval of others. We must sell the idea up to management, or over to coordinates, upstream suppliers, or downstream customers and subordinates.

When you ship your products across town or around the world, thanks to UPS, common-carrier trucking companies and shipping containers, 99% of the time they arrive as they left. How about the shipment of ideas from your head, the pictures you hold in mind, to the mind of your listener? As you ship out your ideas with words, intonation, and gestures, do they always arrive in the mind of the listener as they were pictured in your mind? If so, you had great communication. If not, you had a communication breakdown.

A CALL TO ACTION

Leaders call others to action. This is your job! Your greatest asset as an empowering leader is your set of core beliefs: your commitment to the mission, your passion for the vision, your values and deeply held convictions. These ideals are the standards that guide you in all the decisions you make, one by one, day by day, hour by hour, and moment by moment. As an empowering leader, you create a fully engaged, highly motivated team that rallies around these ideals, by communicating how their contribution ties to the ongoing mission, vision, and values of the organization.

Do more than enlist the cooperation of your associates. Inform them of planning and proposed actions; let them feel part of decision-making. Invite creative ideas and solutions; welcome their input. Invest them with a sense of their value, their contribution, their place in the big picture. Enthusiasm is contagious. Infect every team member with your own enthusiasm and commitment. Capture their imagination, win their hearts, inspire their support.

You will build a team working together creatively and enthusiastically to support the highest aspirations of the organization.

GETTING YOUR IDEAS ACCEPTED

You've come up with a great idea. Unfortunately, it's not

within your power to implement it. So you decide to take it to the people who can make it happen. Before you do this, make sure you are prepared to sell the idea effectively.

Many bright ideas are doomed because they are poorly presented. Follow these tips to get your ideas accepted and acted upon:

> *It's not how many ideas you have. It's how many you make happen.*

- ↻ Put the purpose up front. The attending overarching benefits of your proposal should be the first item you cover. This is how you gain favorable attention.

- ↻ Don't wait until you're 15 minutes or five pages into your message to let your manager or team know the benefits—how your idea will support the mission, vision, value of the organization (for example, save money, improve customer service, eliminate errors, improve safety, cut costs, contribute to continuous improvement).

- ↻ Be specific. Don't cloud the issue with vague words and unnecessary background data.

- ↻ Compare, don't knock. Remember, your audience may have a vested interest in the old method and may take negative comments personally.

- ↻ Stress the benefits. Your proposal is a marketing vehicle for selling your idea, not an opinion paper. Make your case using facts and figures that demonstrate savings, increase safety, and improve performance or ease of operation.

- ↻ Acknowledge limitations. Every idea is going to have some drawbacks, require changes or investment. If you can state those shortcomings up front and provide ways to work around them, you won't give ammunition to opponents. Fear and skepticism will be minimized.

COMMUNICATE WITH POWER

Empowering leaders speak from a place of certainty, clarity and personal power. Use the following guidelines to help ensure that you are speaking from a position of strength in your daily communication, and step into your leadership role with confidence and assurance.

POWERLESS ☹	POWERFUL ☺
Complaining—Too hot/too cold; too slow/too fast; too little/too big	Saying nothing
Describing the undesirable situation	Saying what you will commit to doing yourself, or through others, to improve the undesirable situation
Judging and evaluating people without saying anything to make a difference	Listening to others' comments—evoking problem solving and commitment when the speaker is communicating from the powerless position
Criticizing that hurts	Coaching that helps
Gossiping and condemning	Going direct to the person whose behavior you are unhappy with
Hoping and waiting to see if things work out	Requesting action and promising action to ensure things working out
Waiting to know how to do things exactly right	Starting a project without knowing exactly how it will succeed—with a willingness to correct along the way
Ignoring what is working while focusing on what is not working	Acknowledging others for what is working without ignoring what is not working.

OBSERVATIONS OR REQUESTS?

As an empowering leader, you must understand the distinction between observations and requests. So often managers say things like, "It would be nice if you could type these letters today." That is not a request; that is an observation. Don't be surprised when you make observations like that if you don't get the letters you'd like to have typed. "It would be nice" if you received an unexpected inheritance, won a big new customer, doubled your profits. "It would be nice" if you turned reports in on the first of the month, created a new staging area, provided more training for new hires.

So, if you would like to have the letters typed today, say, "I'd like to have these letters typed today. Will you have time to finish them before you leave?" No matter what response you receive, you'll know where you stand, you will live in a world of certainty. Those responses can vary from a rejection, "No, this report takes priority. I won't have time today," or a counter-offer, "I'm not sure when I'll get this report finished. I can promise to have your letters typed by 10:00 tomorrow. I can let you know by 3:00 if I can get them done today," or, better yet, a promise, "Yes, I'll have them for you by 4:00."

Make your requests clear. To ensure honest communication, be sure people know they can deny requests. Allow people to decline when they truly don't have time; allow for a counter-offer. Insist that people make promises. Don't let anyone get away with "trying" to do anything. Committing to "try" is not a commitment. Eliminate the terrible "T" word, *try*, from your and your team's vocabulary.

COMMUNICATING REQUESTS

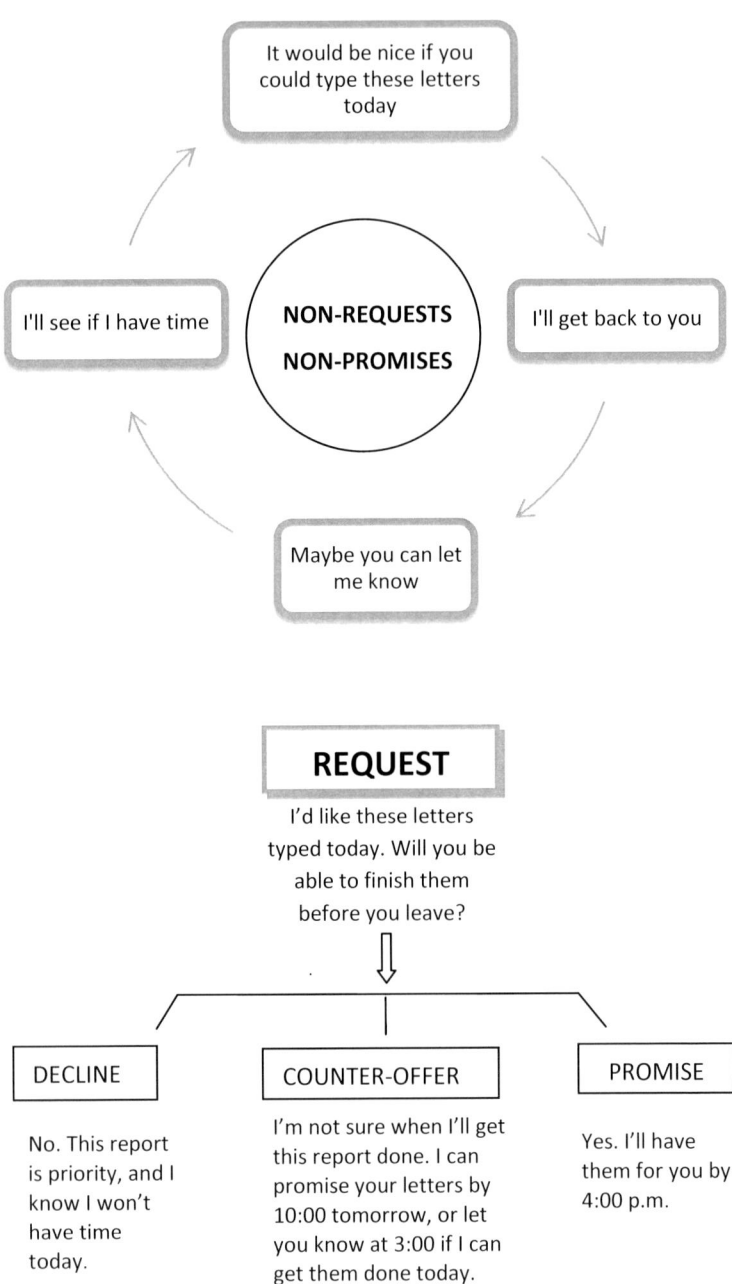

It would be nice if you could type these letters today

I'll see if I have time

NON-REQUESTS
NON-PROMISES

I'll get back to you

Maybe you can let me know

REQUEST

I'd like these letters typed today. Will you be able to finish them before you leave?

DECLINE

No. This report is priority, and I know I won't have time today.

COUNTER-OFFER

I'm not sure when I'll get this report done. I can promise your letters by 10:00 tomorrow, or let you know at 3:00 if I can get them done today.

PROMISE

Yes. I'll have them for you by 4:00 p.m.

CHANGE

As a manager, particularly in this time of accelerated change, you often require associates to make changes, or move from one area of responsibility to another. Even though this move may seem reasonably simple to you, it can be upsetting, discomforting, and challenging for those making the change.

Right Way to Right Size

Bob, coalition leader for a paper mill in northern Ontario, Canada, took quick and positive action in a time of change and uncertainty:

"Recently the mill was downsized due to fiber supply shortages caused by sawmill shutdowns. For this reason, there was a lot of movement of people to different departments and bumping back by seniority. Junior people had to move down and in some cases unfortunately, out. Reassignment movement affecting several departments across the mill can be very complicated. In a union environment, seniority must be respected. What makes things even more complicated is there are three kinds of seniority: company seniority, department seniority, and job seniority. It is complex, hard to understand, and even harder to explain.

"In the restructuring, some people felt that the rules for seniority were not being followed. Things got pretty tense. I noticed that some people were not even talking to each other. Their emotions were running too high. To put it mildly, our operation was no longer working as a team.

"I had two meetings with the department to be sure everyone was included no matter what shift or schedule they were working. I explained to the crews the value of seniority and how it had to be applied consistently over the years. I drew out a sketch of the seniority and bumping process on the whiteboard to help them see and better understand how the whole thing works step-by-step. I visually showed the members how it works in our union, and did a comparison to other unions in the plant.

"After the meetings, the crews seemed okay, now that they had a clear explanation they felt they could trust. The next day, I noticed the people in the department talking to each other again. That was a relief.

Most of the tension seemed to be gone and they were working as a team once again.

↳ *"The lesson I learned from this experience is that when I listen to the concerns of members and explain the ground rules so people can really understand them, most situations are resolved."*

⇆

It really is all about communication. In times of disruptive change and uncertainty, over-communicate! Listen *(Leadership Principle #6 – Be An Active Listener)* to your team members, try and understand their point of view *(Leadership Principle #5 – See Their Point of View)*. Explain any and all changes, the reason for the process, the rule, the standard, or the change. Be sure all the ramifications are clearly understood. Use illustrations, sketches, and where appropriate, analyze and compare to other similar organizations.

SUMMARY

Actions for Empowering Leaders:

↳ Inspire commitment to your mission, vision and values

↳ Step up to the plate with your ideas

↳ Speak from a position of strength

↳ Make clear requests

↳ Tell the why behind the what

The Benefits You Will Gain:

↻ You will have a great sense of achievement

↻ People will respect you and your leadership

↻ You will contribute to continuous improvement

↻ You will know that your ideas make a difference

↻ Your life will be more creative, vital and exciting

Chapter Four

WHAT YOU SAY AND HOW YOU SAY IT

WHAT INFLUENCES JUDGMENT?

As a leader, you are continually being evaluated by your suppliers, customers and associates. They judge you and your organization based on what you say, how you say it, what you do, how you do it, and how you look.

What you say—the words you choose. Words have no inherent meaning. Words are symbols to which we have culturally agreed to assign meaning. As cultures change, so do the meanings of words.

How you say it—the way you emphasize or de-emphasize certain words, your pacing and modulation, can dramatically change the meaning of a word. "Thank you" can range from a sarcastic backhand to a heartfelt, genuine acknowledgement, and it all depends on how you say it.

What you do—showing interest, respect and appreciation; demonstrating authority without ostentation; showing up on time, being the first to say hello, opening the door for others, thumbs up, high five—or, shrugging your shoulders, rolling your eyes, crossing your arms. All these actions influence the judgment of others.

How you do it—walking briskly, sitting up straight, standing erect, getting out from behind your desk and connecting with your associates. Communicating with zeal and excitement, or passive lethargy, influences the judgments people make.

How you look—your personal appearance, "packaging," dress, grooming, an appearance of health and vigor. And just as we judge a book by its cover, people form immediate first impressions largely based on how you look.

1. WHAT YOU SAY

The Words You Choose

How quickly words come and go, and meanings change! Today, there is no "Soviet Union." The former Union is now Russia and several other small, independent nations.

During most of my life, the term "cell" referred to the molecular structure of our body. Today, when we hear "cell," someone is probably referring to a mobile phone.

> *Success in effective presentations doesn't depend on an absence of faults; it depends on an abundance of strengths.*

What about our responses to words that at one time elicited

positive thoughts and emotions, and now they evoke just the opposite? Here's an example:

For several years, my wife Donna Lee was a hospice volunteer. She was required to attend monthly training sessions. At one of her training sessions, another hospice volunteer confided a conversation she had with one of her patients, a terminally ill elderly woman. The patient remarked, "I'll be going home next week." The volunteer understood that meant the woman was going home to die with dignity, surrounded by family and loved ones. Sympathetically, she said, "I'm sorry."

The woman replied, "It's okay, I have aides." Hearing this, the hospice volunteer's heart broke. She thought, "Oh no, a blood transfusion must have been contaminated. Instead of helping this dear old lady, now she has AIDS!" As the volunteer struggled to contain her emotions, the patient continued, "One will come in the morning, and another in the afternoon."

What a relief! The elderly woman didn't have the horrific "AIDS" virus—she had "*aides*" coming to assist her at home. Two words that sound the same, but what a dramatic difference in their meaning!

⇤⇥

The editor of a client's newsletter once enlisted my help in wording an announcement. She and I worked on every word, phrase and punctuation mark. Frankly, it sounded pretty good to me before we started! It was just a short paragraph, less than 75 words. We worked on it for over 30 minutes. By the time we finished, it had a crispness, a punch, an energy we were proud of. It was far better than before we started.

The lesson I learned in this case is that every word matters. And with some pivotal words, the slightest change can make a major difference in the impact, import and significance of my message.

⇤⇥

Using Pictorial Language

When you communicate, you are always limited by your vocabulary and that of your listeners. Using jargon or slang that is outdated or inappropriate weakens your communication. Words that have special meaning for you may turn the other person off, make them more or less receptive to your message. Look for and find words which convey the most precise message. Mark Twain said the difference between a word and the right word is the difference between lightning and a lightning bug.

I spent part of my childhood in the boot-heel of southeastern Missouri—Poplar Bluff and Fisk, to be specific. I loved the summer nights, especially after the 100-degree days. My two younger brothers and I would catch lightning bugs and put them in a Mason jar to watch them flicker. I still associate the smell of honeysuckle with those sultry summer nights.

When I close my eyes, I can hear the creak and squeak of the old porch swing and see the flicker of lightning bugs dancing in the dew-covered honeysuckle. I can see the heavens slashed with stabs of dry heat lightning. The brilliant, bluish-purple flash in the dark night sky, and after a long pause, the loud clap of thunder.

One summer night, a lightning bolt struck my grandmother's beloved weeping willow tree. That great giant had shaded more than half of the backyard for years. In a split second, the lightning sheared it to a fraction of its former size. The lightning bugs my brothers and I caught were powerless compared to the strength of lightning like the bolt that shattered my grandmother's willow. Your well-chosen, vividly descriptive words, compared to just plain everyday words, can make this same dramatic difference in impact.

See how detail brings this story to life:

"I rode my motorcycle home from work every morning," Dennis related, "passing my buddy working at a gas station at 19th and Jefferson Street.

"One morning I was flying up the street when out from behind a city bus came a VW Bug, straight at me. I was probably going 40 mph when I broadsided that little blue Bug just behind the driver's side door. The impact popped every window out of the car.

"My buddy at the gas station heard the rumble of my motorcycle and looked up just in time to see my body catapult through the air as high as the ARCO sign on the corner. He just knew I was dead when I landed in a heap in the service station driveway. For two days I lay unconscious in the hospital. I awoke with a start, thinking I had missed my wedding, which was still a month away. It wasn't until I walked down the aisle on my wedding day that I realized how close I came to missing not just my wedding day, but the rest of my life."

A Ray of Sunlight

Empowering leaders have learned that great communication is like a ray of sunlight. The more you concentrate it, the greater its impact. Often, the fewer words we use, the more impacting those words can be.

> *The Lord's Prayer has 56 words;*
>
> *Lincoln's Gettysburg Address has 266 words;*
>
> *The Ten Commandments, 297 words;*
>
> *The Declaration of Independence, 300 words;*
>
> *But, a U.S. Government order setting the price of cabbage had 26,911 words.*

Conclusion: It's not **how much** you say, it's **what** you say that counts!

What Can You Say in Two Minutes?

The spoken word has changed the course of history in less than two minutes. I have heard hundreds of stirring, powerful, impacting talks that were no more than two minutes long. With practice, you, too, can make an impact on your audience in only two minutes.

Study the talk below. Look at the color, listen to the cadence and see the picture. Check for the basics: when, who, where, what, why. You can use details and still get to the point. In fact, appropriate detail helps you get there faster.

Four score and seven years ago (when) our fathers (who) brought forth on this continent (where) a new nation (what), conceived in Liberty, and dedicated to the proposition that all men are created equal (why).

Now we are engaged in a great civil war, testing whether that nation, or any nation, so conceived and so dedicated, can long endure. We are met on a great battle-field of that war. We have come to dedicate a portion of that field, as a final resting place for those who here gave their lives that that nation might live. It is altogether fitting and proper that we should do this.

But, in a larger sense, we can not dedicate—we can not consecrate—we can not hallow—this ground. The brave men, living and dead, who struggled here, have consecrated it, far above our poor power to add or detract. The world will little note, nor long remember what we say here, but it can never forget what they did here. It is for us the living, rather, to be dedicated here to the unfinished work which they who fought here have thus far so nobly advanced. It is rather for us to be here dedicated to the great task remaining before us—that from these honored dead we take increased devotion to that cause for which they gave the last full measure of devotion—that we here highly resolve that these dead shall not have died in vain; that this nation, under God, shall have a new birth of freedom—and that government of the people, by the people, for the people, shall not perish from the earth.

- Abraham Lincoln, Gettysburg, PA, November 19, 1863

Think of the number of lives that have been impacted by

these few words, a presentation that lasted less than two minutes! Ask yourself, "What can I learn from this talk? Why has this presentation remained a strong influence for over a hundred years?"

↤↦

2. How You Say It

Your Delivery Does It

As an empowering leader, an important part of your job is to persuade others. You must be alert, alive, awake yourself. Speak with sincerity and excitement, so that your listeners know you believe every word you say. Even if you feel it deeply, if you don't seem warm, friendly, enthusiastic and firm, you fail to fully communicate successfully.

Real communication requires that you be willing and able to help your listener empathize with you. Communication is not a cold, logical transfer of information between two machines. You are not Star Trek's "Dr. Spock" or "Data." Your message is filtered by feelings and emotions. You must make a connection with your listeners on a deep, personal, emotional level. You do this by letting your conviction, fervor, excitement, and passion show in your voice and through your words to sweep your listeners up and carry them with you.

At a meeting at the Hilton Hotel with about 500 business managers and owners from the greater Portland area, I sat through a presentation by the vice president of a prominent national bank. The presenter had important information about economic forecasts for the next 12 months that should have been of interest to his listeners. Here was a real opportunity for this executive to make a good impression for his bank, and he blew it. Instead of sitting attentively, eagerly leaning forward, I watched many people in the audience stand up and leave. A gentleman sitting to my right turned to me and said, "It's a good thing it's raining outside or this would really be dry."

Conscious Choice

Your delivery has a significant impact on your communication. Research shows that more than half your personal impact is determined by your delivery: how you speak, the use of your voice, modulation, pitch, and pacing. 90 out of 100 people in crowded professions never rise above mediocrity because they give no time and attention to the development of a well-modulated voice.

> *Your voice is the instrument on which you play the symphony of your life.*

Your voice is inherited. How you use it is up to you. You decide! You have a choice. If you choose to change, and are willing to work at it, you can. You can deliberately make your message and your presence more impacting by developing the effective use of your voice. Who can forget President Reagan before the Berlin Wall, leaning forward, looking intensely straight into the camera, saying forcefully and with slow, deliberate emphasis:

"Mr. Gorbachev, *Tear...down...this...wall!*"

How did you decide what pace to use, how often to pause, whether to drop the end of your sentences or end with a lift? How did you decide whether to speak in incomplete or run-on sentences? When did you decide what speed to speak— to race along, leaving your listeners behind, or go so agonizingly slow that your listeners are bored to tears? The answer, in most cases, is purely by accident. Most of us speak at about the same rate and in about the same manner as our parents, and it has nothing to do with our genes. We are simply modeling our parents' manner of delivery.

Where is your emphasis? Do you over-use certain words or phrases? Are you a flat Johnny One Note? Do you let your sentences run downhill? Do you slur or clip your words? Abraham Lincoln liked to lie on his back and read aloud into a book to develop his diction. Today, you can record your voice, and hear how your presentation sounds!

Winston Churchill, the greatest orator of the 20th century, began his career with a severe speech impediment, a slurring lisp. He acted decisively and worked to overcome it. After many years, he finally stated triumphantly, "My impediment is no hindrance." He turned his biggest liability into his greatest asset.

$$\leftrightarrow$$

The Power of the Pause

When you want to be powerful, pause. Your willingness, your ability to pause at the end of a sentence and allow for silence shows confidence. Learn to use the pause as a conscious skill. When you pause, you give yourself time to think about what you're going to say next. Plus, your message has time to sink in with your listeners. Charles de Gaulle stated, "Silence is the ultimate weapon of power."

Non-words

Punctuating communication with non-words—*er's, ah's, eh's, uh's and ums; the you knows, okays, and Right's!*—signals a lack of confidence, poor preparation and unclear thinking. Non-words are just distracting pause fillers. Get rid of them. Don't be afraid of silence. Discipline yourself to consciously create a pause of two or three seconds. At first you will feel the pauses are excruciatingly long. People say that a three-second pause can feel like thirty; actually most pauses are less than half a second. Practice extending them; when you hear yourself on a recording, your pauses will sound natural.

↤↦

3. WHAT YOU DO

Mannerisms

We tend to assume communication is spoken or written, yet facial expressions, handshakes, all mannerisms are distinct modes of communication which, if not managed, can lead to miscommunication.

Think about your body language. What message do you send if you fold your arms or wring your hands? Folding your arms could indicate defensiveness or a lack of openness; wringing your hands might signal worry or fearfulness. Notice your shrug, a smile or a frown. Make sure your words and actions match. If your words say, "*I like you,*" don't back away. If you say, "*Welcome. Come on in,*" don't look at your watch. Be very careful about pacing back and forth.

Make eye contact. William Blake said, "The eyes are the windows to the soul." Shifty eyes destroy trust and turn people away. Looking away from your listeners, gazing over their heads or admiring the shine on your shoes displays a lack of self-confidence or lack of conviction. You have heard people say, "Can you look me straight in the eye and say that?" The person who does not make good eye contact demonstrates a lack of credibility.

↤⇄↦

A Hand Up

The question always comes up, "What do I do with my hands?" Open them up, reaching out to your audience; show how wide, how tall. Use your fingers to indicate the count. It's hard to climb the ladder of success with your hands in your pockets! Keep your hands away from your pockets, particularly if you have change in them. Jingling change can be an extreme distraction. Avoid planting your hands on your hips, or concealing them with your arms folded over them.

The truth is, if you are too aware of your hands when you are speaking, you may be focusing on yourself rather than on your audience. If you concentrate on your audience and on your message, chances are your hands will move naturally to help you make your point.

↤⇄↦

4. How You Do It

Add Power to Your Presentation

Is there a "theater of excitement" in your personal presentation? I have heard that when Frank Sinatra simply came into a room, all heads turned. To communicate conviction, commitment or determination, use appropriate animation. When in doubt, stand up. Don't be afraid to wave your hands! When you stand in front of a group, let yourself go. When you let yourself loosen up physically, you loosen up mentally and emotionally. You can express excitement, intensity and joy.

For most of us it feels awkward to use expressive gestures and animation. Yet it is necessary to stretch beyond your natural comfort zone if you're going to increase your effectiveness. Gestures loosen you up and help you become more relaxed. The tension goes right out of your fingertips as you raise your hands in the air to show how high you went, or as you lower your body to show how low you were, or as you lean to the right to express the speed of the vehicle that went past. Before a group, always gesture larger than you would one-on-one.

The emotional effect that gestures have on listeners can be dramatic. Just think about some of the world's greatest presenters. The use of natural, spontaneous, forceful gestures always contributes to their impact.

⇥

Animation Conveys Conviction

Gary livens up the evening classes with animated instruction:

"I was bored to tears with the deadpan instructors for our Refrigeration Service Engineers Society night classes. After several weeks, I finally stood up at a monthly planning meeting and said, 'We need to find a way to enliven our night classes. After all, our students have been working all day and they are tired. We owe it to them to make our training sessions lively, stimulating and interesting.' Several members challenged me to do a better job: 'If you're so good, do it yourself.' So I studied, passed all the tests, completed all the paperwork necessary to get my state certificate, and began to teach. Teaching night classes to mechanics who had already worked eight to ten hours that day, I realized I needed to do something different to keep their attention. I developed my own style of animated instruction, and I continued to teach the heat pump classes for eight fun-filled years. I trained over 100 mechanics during those years.

↳*"The lesson I learned from this experience is that being a good teacher, instructor or trainer requires that I must, as Ralph Waldo Emerson said, 'Do nothing ordinary.' I must dramatize my ideas (Leadership Principle #9)."*

HOW YOU LOOK

"Exhibit A"

You and I are always "Exhibit A." Whether others should or should not judge us by our appearance is not the question. We all make immediate judgments based largely on how people look. How else would you form impressions of others? For this reason, it is important to give continuous attention to your packaging—your appearance. How you look as you stand before others—customers, suppliers, fellow employees, management and staff—is a subject of importance to professional leaders. Remember, first impressions are based largely on your appearance.

We all know that first impressions are lasting; you never get a second chance to make a first impression. People may change their minds about you, and often do, and yet they never forget that initial encounter. It will serve you well to be conscious of the impression you're making when you meet a new employee, greet a new supplier, start a new job and are introduced to new people who will be working with or for you.

What do you say with your attire? John Malloy's research, as published in *Dress for Success*, documents the resistance or responsiveness of others based on the style and color of the clothes you wear. I am very careful in my choice of my "uniform" for the day. What I wear has very little to do with my personal preferences. Each day as I dress, I consider the people I will be talking to, and my most important meeting of

> *You never get a second chance to make a first impression.*

the day. For example, I have learned not to wear a suit and necktie when I am speaking to a group of primarily male construction or manufacturing supervisors. I wear my most upscale designer clothes when working with architects, designers or advertisers.

Neatness counts. Even the smallest flaws in your appearance will be noticed by someone, and that someone will be distracted. What does your body tone communicate about your level of health and success? How vital and healthy you look can add to or detract from your credibility. It may seem trivial, but a good tan is a great asset.

Of all the things you wear, your facial expression is most important. Notice the person who forgets to smile—what feeling do you pick up from them? Now, what is your response to the person with a warm smiling expression? You reflect the same open response and reception they have given you.

⇄

SUMMARY
Actions for Empowering Leaders:
- ↻ Choose your words wisely for maximum impact
- ↻ Remember the all-powerful pause
- ↻ Use graphic-specific detail and pictorial language
- ↻ Use appropriate gestures and voice inflections
- ↻ Take a good look in the mirror

Benefits You Will Gain:
- ↻ Your message will impact your listeners
- ↻ You will get the results you want, easier and faster
- ↻ Your listeners will be moved by your conviction
- ↻ Your ideas will be accepted
- ↻ You will make a good impression every time

Chapter Five

CONFIDENT COMPETENCE BEFORE GROUPS

OUR GREATEST FEAR

Death. Disease. Plummeting 40,000 feet in an instant to end it all in the gruesome inferno of an airplane crash. Not exactly the kind of stuff we eagerly await. Yet when it comes to real fear—the kind of spine-tingling, mouth-drying, heart-in-your-throat fright that grips and squeezes like a gorilla headlock—nothing holds a candle to the fear of public speaking!

A survey of 3,000 in the Sunday Times of London found that 41% of the respondents listed "public speaking" as their number one fear, while 19% listed "death." The findings have been validated by countless other surveys and studies over the past three decades.

Call it stage fright or performance anxiety, the fear of speaking in public is dreaded like no other dread. This is a fear that knows no age or sexual barriers; it's one that sends butterflies fluttering in the stomach in as high as 80% of the population. In the thousands of Turbo Leadership Lab sessions I have conducted, a high percentage of experienced, otherwise capable leaders become apprehensive at the prospect of giving a group presentation. If you suffer from the same anxiety, I assure you that you are in the mainstream. If you're among the sweaty-palmed masses, you're in good company. Sir Laurence Olivier, Mr. Thespian himself, is said to have been tormented by stage fright for six years. Jovial Willard Scott reportedly isn't so jolly right before show time. He says he fights the jitters every morning. Even the dictator Fidel Castro, with his ever-present hand-rolled smokes, admits to having a fear of public speaking.

Speaking coherently and persuasively in front of large and small groups is a vital skill for an empowering leader. Those who speak well before others, expressing their ideas confidently and competently, are often given disproportionate credit for knowing more than they know; others who lack this ability are often discounted as less capable than they are. Speaking effectively in front of groups has been, is, and always will be, the shortcut to distinction.

"Fear of speaking" holds many otherwise competent managers back. This need not be so. Speaking skills are relatively easy to acquire, once the fear of speaking is controlled. (Notice I said controlled, not banished.)

Stage Fright Converts to Positive Energy

Among the physical manifestations of nervousness can be queasiness we call "butterflies in the stomach." Those butterflies can turn into all-out phobic fear, resulting in heart palpitations, shortness of breath, shaky hands, weak knees and a feeling of impending doom, in as much as 5% of the U.S. population.

You don't want to kill the butterflies! Just get them flying in formation. You want to control, not eliminate, your nervous energy. I have seen many nervous speakers do an excellent job because they believed in their message, and I have seen speakers who stayed too calm; they appeared indifferent, and they bombed.

It can be a good thing to be a little nervous. It can release the adrenaline that gets you "pumped," and shows power and enthusiasm. It's the same as the pre-game jitters of athletes that enables them to perform at a high level, converting nervousness to energy. You too can make the conversion of "stage fright" into positive energy that demonstrates your belief in what you are saying.

↤
↦

Meet the Challenge Head-On

Mike, supervisor for a manufacturing firm, had the jitters before the Leadership LAB:

"Although I'm a newly promoted supervisor, I had been a unit specialist for ten years. For this reason, I felt really comfortable in my expanded leadership position. Yet when I found out I would be attending Turbo's Leadership LAB, I was very nervous! Why? Because I made the mistake of asking people who had participated in our previous company classes how they felt about their experiences in the sessions. They described speaking in front of the group, being way out of their comfort zone. For me, these were horror stories! During the first session of the LAB, I sat in the back with sweaty palms, nervously trying hard not to be noticed.

"After the first session, I realized that I couldn't continue this way for three months. I committed myself to meet the challenge head-on. I forced myself to sit in the front row. I volunteered to go first with my presentations. I challenged myself to get at least one award—and I got that award, too: 'Most Improved.'

"I actually started to look forward to our Wednesday afternoon LAB sessions. With each new presentation, I became more relaxed and the Lab became an enjoyable experience. I am excited about having developed skill in many useful presentation techniques.

↳*"The lesson I learned from this experience is that I need to get out of my comfort zone if I want to grow as a leader. When I exercise the courage required, my confidence grows and my fears disappear."*

↤↦

What Shall I Talk About?

In speaking before groups, it is wise to begin with subjects you are the expert on. Researching and studying your subject can certainly build confidence—the more you know about a subject, the more competent you are. Drawing on personal experience from the laboratory of your own life is the greatest single confidence-builder of all. No one has more expertise on your experiences than you!

> *You are the expert on you.*
> --Lynn Robinson

When you are on the right topic—one you have earned the right to talk about, are an expert on and are excited about sharing, you have the strength of your convictions. If you stray from your own experiences, give your opinions instead of experience, or speak in vague generalities, you run the risk of losing credibility with your audience. Your uncertainty can lead to nervousness and fear. Ask yourself, "Have I proven what I am preparing to say in the "lab" of my life?" If your answer is "Yes," feel and show your confidence. You've earned it.

⇤⇥

On the Spot

Patricia, design engineer for a skylight construction company, ended up with egg on her face:

"My first year out of college, the engineering firm I worked for represented the owner for a project that had started a few months before I joined the firm. It hadn't been decided yet who would be the drafter on the project, so the boss rotated attendees to the weekly project meetings. When it was my turn, I was so excited. I had only been to one project meeting in my career, and this project was for my alma mater. We got to the site office and when everyone arrived, my boss went through the usual pleasantries before saying, 'For those of you who haven't already met her, this is Miss Whitaker. She'll be running the meeting today.'

"My heart stopped; my eyes got as big as fifty cent pieces. I caught my reaction before I made a complete fool of myself. But inside, I had the 'Home Alone' kid expression going on, 'Aghhhhhh! I don't know anything about running one of these meetings! How can he do this to me?' I pulled myself together quickly and got the meeting under way. Just follow the agenda, I told myself. How hard can that be?

"Well, the contractors went off on a tangent on almost every agenda item. I kept glancing at my boss and the client to gauge whether or not the contractors were discussing anything relevant to the item at issue. Poker faces—no help there.

"Eventually, we got through everything on the agenda and I thought, 'Thank you, God, that's over!' As the meeting broke up, I was sure that everyone there could tell I knew nothing about running a project meeting. I had egg all over my face."

⇆

This is a warm, humorous story. You must have laughed as you read it. An empowering leader would never put a team member in this untenable position. Everyone should have adequate notice, training and preparation time before being asked to do any task, especially run a meeting!

It is a good idea, though, for you to be prepared for every eventuality. You may be called on without notice to answer questions, take a part in, or even run a meeting. Following the ideas in THE LANGUAGE OF LEADERSHIP can help you be prepared for whatever challenge comes your way and increase your ability to think on your feet. The world is changing at ever-increasing

> ⋩ *Speaking effectively in front of groups has been, and always will be, the shortcut to distinction.* ⋩

speeds. Of all the qualities a leader must develop, the ability to communicate effectively in group settings is one of the most important.

↤↦

PASSION—ANIMATION—CONVICTION

As a leader, your presentations are for the purpose of getting action. To get action, you must motivate. You must understand, and appeal to, the emotions of your audience. Heart-to-heart is where motivation starts. Talking head-to-head leads to little improvement in performance and has no motivating power.

Ask yourself, "Am I excited when I think about this experience?" If not, then get excited! If you can't get excited, don't waste your listeners' time. Find a topic you can get excited about, then prepare to let your excitement show! Be eager to share. The entire time you are talking, let your natural expressive personality shine out. Your listeners deserve the best of you! Your team, your department, want to believe in you and your ideas. They are inescapably connected to you; they are looking to you for leadership. They know their success depends on you.

When you are passionate about your message and convey your excitement with appropriate animation, you instill conviction in your listeners. In the process your fear takes flight. When your associates are inspired by your passion, you have won their hearts.

As I've coached tens of thousands of speakers, I've watched people who you might otherwise think of as quiet, introverted, or passive. When they get on the right subject, one they are passionate and excited about, one they are eager to share, one from the "lab of their life," suddenly they become animated. Their gestures are natural and spontaneous. There is vocal variety in their delivery. Their volume goes up as appropriate, and down. When they are communicating something of a confidential nature, they achieve the dramatic effect of a stage whisper. And I have watched the audience lean forward, smile, sometimes nod their heads and applaud with great enthusiasm.

⇆

So, How Do I Prepare?

Practice makes perfect. It's more accurate to say practice makes permanent! At the practice range, golfers who slice a bucket of balls have perfected their slice. They have become expert "slicers," not expert golfers. Practice only makes perfect when you practice doing the right things in the right way.

Organize and think through your life experiences before you make your presentation. Analyzing your experience gives you a foundation to build on, leading to a clearer picture of what you want to say. See the scene like a movie on the screen of your mind as it unfolds. This kind of thorough thought gives you greater confidence and helps you develop a laser focus as you drive toward your point.

Analyze Your Experience

When did it happen? Time—date, day, season

Where did it happen? Location–home, work, community, vacation

Who was involved? Key players in your story— friends, family, coworkers

What happened?

Describe the circumstances of the event

Mention the activators that prompted the actions

What was the outcome?

Think It Through

What did you learn from this experience?

Would you do it differently if you had the chance? How?

How does what you learned apply to the present situation?

End on a High Note

Call your audience to action

Promise an important benefit.

⇤

Get To the Point

Some of us need to learn to get to the point. The "three S's" of speaking provide a good guideline to help you make your point: Stand up, Speak out, Sit down.

> ➤ **STAND UP!** By "stand up" we mean, if at all appropriate just that: Stand up. When you are seated you are a voice. When you stand you are a personality. You have a more commanding presence. You and your subject gain appropriate attention.
>
> ➤ **SPEAK OUT!** "Speak out" means to raise your voice to ensure all can hear you. If you are in a large room,

and the group you are speaking to numbers more than 40, I recommend using a microphone. If you are offered a mike, don't say, "I don't need a mike." Yes you do. With a hand-held mike, hold it so it always gently touches your chin. Your added volume, if not overdone, can add an element of authority and conviction that is never present if you are thought to be timid and unsure of yourself.

➢ **SIT DOWN!**—Know your point, get to the point and when you have made your point, sit down. Don't ramble on, repeating yourself, saying the same things or running on with dreary redundancy. Sit down.

Forget Yourself

As you make your presentation, there are three things you can be thinking about: yourself, yourself + your topic, your topic + your audience:

➢ Yourself
   If you are dominated by fear, if you are nervous or anxious when you speak before a group, it is the natural result of thinking about yourself. You are wondering, How do I look? How do I sound? What do they think of me? You are overly "Self"-conscious.

➢ Yourself + Your Topic
   When you are thinking about both yourself and your topic, it can be even worse. Did I get the facts right? Did it flow as I prepared it? What do they think about me? Do I look OK? Do I sound OK? For best results, forget "Your" self and think of:

➢ Your Topic + Your Audience
   Get into your subject with your audience! When your mind and even your heart are focused on how you

can reach, touch, help, and move your audience, everything changes. Now, instead of being "Self"-conscious you are "Others"-conscious.

It's Not About You

It's not about you! Keep the focus on your listeners. Avoid using, "I think;" "I want;" "I believe;" "As far as I'm concerned." Instead, say, "You will find;" "You may have noticed;" "You can see;" "You have probably already found..."

↤↦

The Smile that Refreshes

Imagine that you are speaking to a crowded room of eager listeners. Suddenly your mind goes blank—you forget what you just said, and what comes next. You don't know what to say; you lose your place. You've seen it happen to others. They stammer and sputter and even apologize. What should you do?

"Remain calm, look at your audience, pause and smile." recommends Peter Bender, author of the Canadian best Seller, *Secrets of Power Presentations.* "If you panic, you'll lose your thoughts. When you smile, you look confident; your brain will get back on track."

> ⋛ *It's not how much you have that makes people look up to you, it's who you are.* ⋜
> —Elvis Presley

CREATE RECEPTIVITY

R efer to people in your audience by name as you go along. It's a great way to gain receptivity. Hearing their name is a compliment! It gets the favorable attention of the person whose name you use, and everyone wonders, "Will she call my name next?"

E njoy this opportunity. You can have fun by letting a little "ham" out. Smile. Let your ivories show. Your audience will smile back. This will relax you, and your audience will be more receptive.

C oaching: A trusted friend can be a great source of feedback for improvement. Little tips, ideas, things your coach may spot, help you improve your delivery and arrive at your goal of effectiveness. Coach your coach on the importance of telling you things you do well, not just your faults and shortcomings.

E xhibits can help you secure and retain attention. Exhibits make your presentation engaging, easier to follow and more memorable. (More on props on the following page.)

P raise: Praising your audience for something they have achieved is a great way to start every meeting. Compliment someone for something they have done. There is no better way to create receptivity than to begin with a compliment.

T alk in terms of your audience's interests. Point out the benefits they will gain from following your advice. Answer their "What's in it for me" questions with, "This will help you operate more safely, run faster, improve customer service, increase sales, give you a distinct competitive advantage."

I nability: Don't make excuses—time, health, poor memory, lack of preparation, or distance. Excuses only weaken your delivery. That's a tough act to follow is a left-handed compliment, putting down the other speaker by calling their presentation an "act." It starts you off with a plea for sympathy.

V oice: Warmth and friendliness in your voice will always cause your listeners to be more receptive to your message. Be aware of your pace, vocal variety, pitch, volume, and the power of the pause. (See Chapter Four)

I nvolvement: Get your audience involved. Encourage feedback. Ask for a nod of the head or a show of hands. If you ask for a show of hands, raise your own hand to demonstrate and encourage them to raise theirs.

T hink motivation. Why are you presenting? Ask yourself, what do I want them to do? If you want to motivate others to action, you must be moved and motivated yourself.

Y ou are the message. "Who you are speaks so loudly, I cannot hear what you say." You cannot say one thing and be another. So be yourself; let your own high ideals show clearly. Be what Quintilian, the greatest Greek orator, called "a good man, skilled in speaking."

Following these 11 tips will help you create receptivity—gain an attentive audience, get your message across, and build your own confidence.

᠀

Dress Rehearsal

How Misty, restaurant manager, ended up "dressed in red:"

"I was working for the Colorado Springs Air Academy, where we were making those 'wonderful' airline meals you all love so much.

"I had only been managing for two to three months when the Delta and United's annual food catering contracts came up for renewal. Two top managers were picked (Mike and I) to make our company's presentations to the airlines. We each had a team of five employees and we were to put together a new top-of-the-line menu presentation for the airlines. Mike was to represent United, while I supported Delta.

"Each team had about three weeks to get everything ready, on top of our regular daily duties. About two and a half weeks passed and we were ready, except that as each day passed, I became more and more nervous. I tried not to show it, but my team saw right through me. I remember the night before the presentation competition. I told one of my team members that I really had not prepared myself for the next day. That night, I got about four hours of restless sleep. The next thing I remember was getting awakened by a 5:00 am knock at my door. My whole team was outside, all set to get their captain ready for the big day. First, we went out to breakfast. Then we went shopping, and they bought me a very professional business-like suit. Next, I got my hair and nails done. Finally, 4:30 pm rolled around. It was time to go to the academy to make our presentations.

"All I could remember while I was standing in front of hundreds of people was praying and hoping that I wouldn't mess up. After we gave our presentation, I was so nervous that I had to run to the ladies' room before the judges announced the winning team.

"When I returned, it was time to announce the winner. My Delta team won! I went up to receive the award. Everyone except me noticed that when I came back from the restroom, I had tucked my skirt into my pantyhose. After that, I was known as 'Red.'

↳ *"I learned that my preparation should be complete. My commitment should be to stretching, growing, looking the part and presenting with confidence—doing my very best for myself and my team. If I make mistakes, and who doesn't, I want to make them in the pursuit of excellence and growth."*

⇄

Small, Courageous Steps

Just the act of doing new things—giving a short speech, taking a class, participating in a problem-solving team—can open up many new possibilities and opportunities. Following is another example of someone who stepped out of their comfort zone:

Tom, a production supervisor, learned something new about himself:

"One of our assembly supervisors expressed the desire for a few of her assemblers to learn some of the practical aspects of blueprint reading. Because of my inspection and machining background, my supervisor asked if I would consider conducting a one-time class for about 15 people in that department.

"I don't recall spending much time thinking it over. I didn't like the idea of speaking in front of groups (I'd never tried it, I just knew I wouldn't like it). There were no precedents, guidelines, or materials for such a class. In spite of all that, I agreed to conduct the class. As the date drew near, I started to think, 'Here is another fine mess I have gotten me into.'

"The training class must have gone well, because that one session turned into six classes, totaling about 100 people. By the time I finished, I'd lost most of whatever fear I had of public speaking. In fact, I found out that I actually enjoyed it.

"Next, I took a company sponsored on-site class called Interpersonal Communication, where I learned additional points about speaking. This confirmed for me that I would like to do more instruction. As a direct result of the communications class, where the 'right' person happened to hear me speak, I was asked if I would like to become a Certified Company Facilitator. I jumped at the chance! Three years ago I probably would have declined, but now I was ready.

↳ *"I have learned from this experience that even very small courageous steps forward can lead to more growth, fun and progress."*

PROPS SUPPORT YOUR MESSAGE

If you have ever been responsible for giving presentations to any size group, you know the importance of good visual aids. Research from the U.S. Public Health Service audio visual facility shows that when people are taught *by words alone*, their immediate recall of the material is around 70%. Three days later they only remember less than 10%. This is a problem. When people both **hear** and **see** information, their immediate recall is 85%. After three days they still retain up to 65%!

So, a good rule is, never make a presentation empty-handed. Enhance your message with the effective use of good visual aids. What makes a "good" visual aid? A good visual aid is one that effectively enhances the point you are making. Props can help you secure eye control, which is the first step to mind control. Mind control leads to data control, getting new information into your listener's mind.

Examples of props are pictures, trophies, graphs, news articles, certificates, sketches, Power Points, line graphs, trend and Pareto bar charts.

Always remember that visual aids are just that—aids. The reason for using visual aids is to enhance your verbal presentation, not to replace it; to add to, rather than detract from. Imagine what you would do if your PowerPoint broke down. Could you still make an effective presentation? If not, you may be relying too much on your visuals.

Using Props Effectively

P **Props** can help you effectively gain and retain attention. Your prop can be your proverbial "two by four." Your prop makes your presentation more memorable. Your message will stick in your listener's mind.

R **Raise** your prop high, higher than seems natural to you. Hold it steady, parallel to the floor, in plain view where everyone can see it.

O **Obstruction:** Your prop can become an obstruction if you hide behind it or turn your back to the audience to look at the prop. When using a Power Point, always use a laser pointer, hold it steady and move it slowly. Stand as close to the screen as practical so your audience can see both you and your slides.

P **Preparation** allows you to talk to your audience, not to the prop. If you plan to use a flip chart, consider writing as much as possible on it before you begin. If you need help with your prop, make the assignment early, before you begin. Get technical help— beforehand! Eighty percent of Power Point presentations I see are delayed for technical reasons.

S **Support:** Your prop, correctly used, supports you and your point. It acts as a form of evidence, making your presentation more credible and convincing. Props can help you get your mind off yourself and feel more confident and comfortable in front of the group.

When you are finished, **set your prop down**. Don't fumble around with it. Put it away. Turn off the Power Point, and get the attention back to what you are saying, the point you are there to make, the action you want your audience to take.

MAKING INTRODUCTIONS

You may think you will never be called on to introduce a speaker in front of a group. First of all, "never" is a long time; secondly, every time you introduce a new supplier or a new employee to one or more people, you are in fact making an introduction.

A good introduction is a pep talk for the speaker.

Your introduction plays a significant role in the way an individual is received, and sets the stage for future interactions. You are responsible for the first impression that is being made. When done well, your introduction will go a long way toward ensuring a quick start, a good start, for the speaker. A good introduction is a pep talk for the speaker. Selling the speaker captures attention and ensures a good reception from listeners. If you do your job well, by the time you are through, they are on the edge of their chairs, eagerly looking forward to what the speaker has to say. So you will want to make certain your introductions are well prepared and well delivered.

Lousy Introductions

Many years ago, when working in Rockford, Illinois, I agreed to make a presentation for the Caterpillar Equipment dealers of Southern Illinois. Because of my busy schedule, Caterpillar arranged for a private airplane to fly me from Rockford to an airfield where someone from the dealers association met me and rushed me over to the Holiday Inn where the meeting was being held, with less than 30 minutes to spare. A few minutes after we were seated, the program chairman "introduced" me. I almost wished we had taken a wrong turn in our haste to reach the hotel on time. He said, "I'm not quite sure where we found this fellow, I'm not altogether sure what he's going to talk about. By the way, what is your name?"

I walked to the podium, thinking that, without question, a new record had just been set for the worst introduction I have ever received.

Well, it happened again. I made special schedule arrangements to give a talk for the managers of a fast-growing refuse firm in Tacoma, Washington. My associate and I left Portland at about 2:00 pm so we could be in Tacoma early for my 6:30 pm presentation. We had made extra efforts to prepare the custom handouts, and I had completed the due diligence needed to be sure I knew the group's makeup and everything I could learn about the nature of their unique business, sales trends, and customers.

The way I was introduced was lousy! It seemed the person who introduced me had not talked to the company's comptroller who arranged for me to speak. He didn't have my biography; he really didn't know my topic. He had no idea how my presentation was designed to create value for their team.

The lesson I learned is to make certain that introductions are well presented, designed to prepare the audience to benefit, and ensure the enthusiastic reception of the presenter.

⇆

Compare these introductions to the one Chuck made:

Off the Charts!

At straight up 12:00 noon, Chuck introduced me to the downtown Portland B.Y.U. Management Society. I've been introduced to thousands of audiences across this country and around the world in ways that range from too formal to too casual, from nonplused to motivated. Chuck's introduction was (on a scale of one to ten) a 15. It was off the charts! He told about my professional background, my experience, his personal experience in my training, and then he said something that I don't recall ever hearing before. He said, "When I talked to Larry's wife, she told me...," and he went on to talk about my integrity. When I stood up to make my presentation, I had tears in my eyes. I was motivated to perform at the highest possible level I could for this group.

⇆

How to Introduce a Speaker

So, what makes a good introduction? Whether it's a formal occasion or a company team meeting, here is a simple 3-step formula that you can follow to generate interest among the audience, provide a pep talk for the speaker, and build your confidence. Use these guidelines to build your own enthusiasm and the enthusiasm of the person you are introducing. Your meeting will run smoothly, and you'll make a great personal impression.

"SBQ" Formula for Introducing a Speaker:

'*S*'ubject; '*B*'enefits; '*Q*'ualifications

Subject:

A simple statement of the subject of the presentation is all that is needed—one line, something like: "Our subject tonight is 'Catching More Catfish,' or 'Cutting Down on Box Cutter Accidents,' or 'Keeping an Eye on Eye Injuries,' or 'Turning Around Night Shift Turnover,' or 'Moving Morale Up,' or 'Productive People Practices.'" This is your attention-getter. It should gain attention and arouse some curiosity and interest.

Benefits:

Spell out, for everyone to understand, the benefits they individually, or as a group, will gain by listening to and acting on the ideas they are about to hear: "By listening carefully to our speaker, you will be able to . . ." To drive home the benefit, use transition statements such as "enabling you to . . ."or, "so that . . . .,"or, "This will help you . . . . ."

You are not giving the talk; you are selling the benefits the listeners will gain from the speaker's presentation.

Qualifications:

Establish credibility. Here is where you use the speaker's background, education, training and prior experience to sell the audience on listening. Create a commonality of experience, the things the speaker has in common with your audience. Mentioning your relationship with the speaker goes a long way toward creating rapport.

The final words of your introduction are the speaker's name. Lift your voice and punch out their last name. This is your mini-pep talk for the speaker. It pumps them up and lifts them out of their chair.

On-Boarding

Introducing new team members is an important part of on-boarding. Your on-boarding responsibility begins the day you hire an associate to fill a new or existing role. You have just made one of the most important decisions managers ever make. What will determine this new team member's success, the achievement of the objectives you hired them to accomplish? Assuming the role is well defined with clear objectives and that you made a good hire, the remaining determining factors are how well you train the new hire and how quickly they are accepted and supported by the present team.

Let's remember people have a natural curiosity and skepticism, and if left to their own devices, tend to be negative. Don't leave it up to new people to have to "prove" themselves. Too much nonproductive energy is wasted in the process.

You have a responsibility to effectively introduce the new team member into the work culture in such a manner that "proving" themselves is no longer necessary. Instead, everyone's confidence is at an all-time high. This can be done by:

You can ramp up their acceptance and ensure a quick start by following these "SEES" guidelines:

"SEES"

Everyone *"SEES"* where we are heading.

'S' *tart* by establishing with the entire team the results expected with the new team member. Explain the goal to be achieved (cutting costs, improving efficiency, increasing sales, heightening customer satisfaction, etc.).

'E' *stablish* a commonality of experience, interest, education, and background. This is the personal touch (families, hobbies, community involvement, outside interests).

'E' *stablish* each party, all team members, as experts and achievers by reviewing the track record of accomplishments (existing team members' recent achievements, new team members' success in their former position).

'S' *tate* your high expectations in positive, energetic goal-oriented terms ("by working together, we will be able to _____"). This is where you raise the banner once again. Talk about your mission, vision, values and goals for the year ahead.

When you take the time to introduce new team members carefully, thoughtfully everyone **"SEES"** the addition as a win for the team!

SUMMARY
Actions for Empowering Leaders

- ↻ Volunteer to lead or speak in front of groups
- ↻ Choose a subject that draws on your life experience
- ↻ Get excited about your subject
- ↻ Use props to strengthen your presentation
- ↻ Be thoughtful when preparing introductions

The Benefits You Will Gain:

- ↻ Your fears will disappear
- ↻ You will be exhilarated by getting your point across successfully
- ↻ You will capitalize on all your training and experience
- ↻ You will earn respect
- ↻ Your career will advance at an ever-increasing speed

Chapter Six

BETTER, SHORTER MEETINGS

"A MEETING IS A MEETING IS A MEETING"

Ken, distribution center manager of a regional mass merchandiser, came to me at the close of a leadership training session and said,

"You know, Larry, I've been with my firm for over 23 years. I've been the manager of our distribution center for over 13 years. Since you conducted the Leadership Team Advance for our key management team, it's been like working at a different company.

"As an example," Ken said, "for my whole career, I've hated attending meetings. I thought they were a waste of time. Now, I'm showing up at meetings I'm not even invited to."

So, to say that a meeting is a meeting is a meeting is not true. It may be true that most of us have attended far more nonproductive meetings than productive ones.

Making Meetings Productive

Meetings are an important tool for any group of people working together. They are a vehicle to problem-solve, celebrate, plan, and make commitments that alter the future. Team meetings can reinforce understanding, and emphasize the need to meet deadlines. Meetings do not need to be lengthy or formal. It is possible to get more accomplished in a 10-minute standup meeting in the warehouse at the beginning of the shift than in a 3-hour executive meeting in the boardroom. The success of the meeting depends on who's running it, not the "importance" of the participants. The empowering leader uses the right combination of meetings on a regular basis to provide structure to the work environment and intentionally shape the conversations that make up the culture of the organization.

Making a meeting productive takes a good deal of self-discipline. First, determine what kind of meeting is appropriate, and then stick to your plan. End your meeting as soon as its purpose has been accomplished. Every minute counts for your associates. They have work to do. Don't raise additional or off-point matters for discussion. Sum up and adjourn.

Numerous studies of the manager's workday have found that managers at every level are in a meeting of some sort more than half of every business day. Many managers and supervisors resent meetings and see them as a non-productive waste of time.

Conversation, even communicating with only one other

person can be called a meeting. If you are to be effective, your every meeting must be purposeful, not a bull session.

↤↦

Rigid Meeting Manager

When Turbo Leadership Systems accepted an assignment with a corporation of about 1200 associates at their primary site, we began by sitting in to observe their morning production meeting, and were later invited to visit their quarterly goal-setting session.

We saw many opportunities for improvement in both meetings. We heard a lot of grumbling: too many people; redundant; rehashing the same old problems over and over; looking backward with no clear action assignments or accountability for the future. Many opportunities to stop waste, speed up the process, and improve safety and quality were missed.

The senior managers who were required to attend the quarterly goal-setting meeting liked the idea of goal-setting. They just didn't feel that what happened in the meetings helped with alignment, focus, or clarity. Their meetings didn't result in the engagement needed to create the breakthroughs they all wanted.

Our Leadership Team Advance (LTA) offsite created an opportunity for peers to critique the effectiveness of the plant manager who oversees the daily morning production meeting. Everyone gave his morning meeting poor ratings. As part of the peer input, this manager received a number of recommendations about how he could improve his production meeting. He developed an action plan for implementing many of their suggestions and promised to make immediate changes.

To our astonishment, within a matter of days he had "re-surveyed" his peers and decided not to make any of the agreed-to changes in his morning production meeting! This is an amazing example of dogged resistance to change, the human determination to maintain the status quo, the difficulty in changing cultural norms.

↰

In *What Makes an Effective Executive*, the late Peter Drucker commented that great leaders may be charismatic or dull, generous or tight-fisted, visionary or numbers-oriented. What makes them effective is that they all follow certain basic practices:

> They ask, "What needs to be done?"
> They ask, "What is right for the enterprise?"
> They develop action plans
> *And they run productive meetings.*

↰

Seven Essentials for Productive Meetings

Follow these seven steps to make your next meeting productive:

- ↻ Define your purpose
- ↻ Determine who needs to attend
- ↻ Set your agenda
- ↻ Make meetings efficient: start on time, stop on time
- ↻ Stay on track

○ End with agreed-to action assignments

○ Keep records

1. **Define your purpose**, the reason for the meeting. Saying "communication" isn't enough. Get more specific. What results, what improvements, do you want from this meeting? One of the worst reasons to schedule a meeting is because "we have always done it." Some of the best reasons for meetings are to follow up on commitments, solicit information, answer questions, look at the score, brainstorm for improvement, solve problems, celebrate success, sell an idea and include your team in decision-making. A meeting without a specific purpose is a waste of time. Discontinue any regularly scheduled meetings when they no longer serve their original purpose. State the purpose of the meeting up front each time you meet. If your only reason for meeting is to give people information they already have, don't meet.

2. **Determine who needs to attend** to insure the desired result! Excuse anyone who isn't in a position to contribute to the desired result or outcome of the meeting.

3. **Set your agenda.** People have at least 2,000 pet peeves about meetings. The top three are: They don't know why they're required to be there, there's no meeting focus, and nothing changes as a result of the meeting. Good agendas help solve these problems. An agenda is essential because it puts you in control of the meeting. It is your road map to accomplishment. Distribute the agenda before the meeting so all participants know what to expect and

come prepared. State each agenda item as specifically as you can. Instead of "Let's talk about the budget," ask, "How can we reduce our budget by 10%?" If you're not specific, some may come prepared to tout ways to increase the budget or look for different ways to spend the current budget. With a specific action item, everyone is focused on the same issue, looking for the answer to the same question.

Set a time limit for each agenda item. You can say, "We need a decision on this in 10 minutes. That means we'll explore options for nine minutes, and then follow with a vote." Then stick to the time limit. It is useful to structure meetings so important topics are given sufficient attention.

4. **Make meetings efficient**. No one should have to suffer through ineffective meetings. Have your company mission, vision, values, meeting ground rules, and code of conduct on the wall of all meeting rooms. Ask for the behaviors necessary to improve meeting effectiveness.

   When you lead meetings, a few simple steps will help you feel in control: Take time before the meeting to gather your thoughts. To free you to focus on the direction and dynamics of the meeting, ask a trusted scribe or secretary to write down the key points and action agreements.

5. **Stay on track.** Empowering leaders structure their meetings so everyone participates without being put abruptly on the spot. An effective leader includes everyone in the meeting, so the good ideas of the shy team members are not overlooked because more

talkative people dominate. People are energized when they participate rather than merely observe. Meetings are a rare opportunity for the team to really experience "team."

Make sure people don't interrupt. Learn to gently steer associates back to the business at hand when they start talking about issues that side-track your meeting. One technique is to have a flip chart pad headed "the bin" or "parking lot." If people start to wander, say "Let's put that in the bin," and write it down for future discussion.

6. **End with decisions**, agreed-to actions and accountability. There are a lot of unfinished meetings floating around. Meetings begin when someone decides a group must get together to do something. They're not over until the objectives are met. A key part of any meeting is the list of agreements that "make real" the good ideas discussed during the meeting. Decide what must be done next, by whom and by when. Assign timelines to each commitment as it is made.

7. **Keep records.** Take official minutes; they come in handy and help to avoid confusion. At the end of the meeting, post an email to all participants with the list of commitments for everyone to refer to. Then follow up to make sure the assigned person is held accountable. Begin each subsequent meeting by celebrating achievements and reviewing outstanding promises. Incomplete agreements need to be quickly recommitted to with new timelines.

21 Rules for Productive Meetings

Before the meeting:

1. Clearly define the purpose of the meeting.
2. Explore the alternatives—do we really need to meet? Will meeting save time?
3. When possible, hold stand-up meetings.
4. Keep the number of participants appropriate.
5. Choose an appropriate time.
6. Choose an appropriate place—a central location free from outside distractions, properly equipped, with scoreboards, whiteboards, and easels with flip chart pads.
7. Your regular team meeting room should be clean, free of clutter and distractions. Having your mission, vision and values clearly displayed on the wall provides a visual context for the meeting.
8. Establish time limits.
9. Assign a timekeeper and a keeper of the minutes.

During the meeting:

10. Start on time.
11. Open with inspiration. Read the mission of your organization or department, or the purpose of the group.
12. Stick to the agenda.
13. Report on the achievement of former assignments.
14. Discuss goal projections.
15. Control interruptions.
16. Accomplish the purpose of the meeting.
17. Restate decisions and accepted assignments.
18. End on time.

After the meeting:

19. Use a scheduled meeting critique checklist. (See "My Meeting Critique," p 125)
20. Expedite the preparation and distribution of commitments and minutes.
21. Ensure progress reports are made on decisions.

EVERYONE LOVES A STORY

In the Leadership LAB we create opportunities for class members to tell stories about risks they took that paid off, a time they got egg on their face, something at work that made them mad. As class members share their experiences, we often hear stories of things that resulted either in an injury or came close; clear examples of unsafe behavior, an accident or a near miss.

Many "safety meetings" are hardly safety meetings at all. They seem to consist almost exclusively of platitudes, childish chides and haranguing lectures. These personal, real-life stories would be marvelous for a safety meeting. Great stories, far more powerful than mere statistics, reading from a manual, seeing a video or the all-too-common platitudes, clichés and preachments. I've asked not once, not a dozen times, but hundreds of times, "Have you ever used that story as a part of a safety meeting?" I can honestly say I have never heard a "yes!"

The value of stories is not sufficiently appreciated. We all respond to stories, we remember stories, we get the point of stories. Stories have convincing credibility. Stories penetrate our psyche; they influence our values, judgments and behaviors. Stories can be just as available and as powerful for you as they were to Uncle Remus, Mark Twain, Abraham Lincoln or Ronald Reagan.

So, be on the lookout for stories and examples to enliven your meetings. Remember to go back through your own experience to find stories that make your point. Be alert for illustrations and examples of great customer service, and the empowered or disempowered employees you encounter. Make it a personal project to look for stories you can use to help your presentation come alive, add credibility, and make your meetings more enjoyable. You may be amazed at how many colorful examples you have been letting slip right through your fingers. Grab them, make note of them on 3x5 cards, make them a part of your repertoire, use them in future production, safety, planning, or monthly meetings.

$$\leftrightarrows$$

USING FLIP CHARTS

Graphics help. Flip charts with your diagrams help team members relate to quality and efficiency, sales, costs, and safety performance. A hardy easel with a flip chart pad belongs in every meeting room. With a flip chart, you can create visuals that will help you get the attention of everyone at your meetings. This helps engage their minds, and ultimately they leave knowing what you want them to know. You can highlight key points as well as respond to and capture input from the group. You can tear off sheets and stick them up on the wall as you go along. A white board does not allow for this flexibility. At the conclusion of the meeting you can gather the sheets and type them up as a record of your meeting results.

Here are some tips for using your flip chart pad:

- Write out key points to help the team gain information quickly and easily.
- Print in large block letters 1 to 2 inches in height. If your group is large or your room is deeper than 30 feet, print larger and bolder

- ↪ Don't talk to the easel board while writing on it
- ↪ Don't put more than about 10 lines of information on any given page
- ↪ Wait at least 20-30 seconds after you finish writing before you flip the page. Better yet, tear off the page and tape it to the wall.
- ↪ Don't stand in front of the easel after you have finished writing

Flip Chart + Brainstorm + Action = Success

Jim, IT manager for a trucking parts company, used brainstorming to motivate his team to action:

"On my way back to the office after the leadership training session, I stopped by an office supply store and purchased a flip chart and an easel to use for our department meetings. That afternoon I called a special department team meeting for Thursday morning.

"I explained the nine rules for brainstorming (p 122). I displayed on my flip chart the sheet of ideas I brought back, and described the process I had experienced. Then I wrote on a fresh page, 'In what ways can we clean up our computer room—and keep it clean?' I started the stopwatch and we brainstormed for six minutes. To my surprise, we were able in those six minutes to generate 26 pretty good ideas. Some were off-the-wall—like 'burn it!' but even those suggestions had value because they added the light touch we needed to be creative and spontaneous—to free ourselves from conventional thinking.

From our list of 26 suggestions, we identified with a voting process the 'hot ideas'—where we could get the most 'bang for the buck.' Everyone voted for their top three.

"Then, without any further input from me, people volunteered to immediately take action on some of our listed items. Scott's idea was to have a mass cleaning of the computer room. The next day, Friday, we all wore our jeans and tennies. Ron arranged for lunch—a pizza delivery. Loaded with carbohydrates, we attacked the computer room with zeal. People paired up in little teams to throw out junk, sort out the obsolete from the useable and organize what was left. We worked steadily until the computer room was clean. By 3:30, we were exhausted, dirty and satisfied with a job well done. The team awarded me an old nylon attaché case they unearthed—my trophy for pioneering the change. The following Wednesday morning we held our team meeting in our new space, the cleaned-out computer room.

"The $249 I invested in the easel has already paid for itself many times over. *

↳ *"The lesson I learned from this experience is that power and energy rise when I ask the team to brainstorm for ideas."*

> *Note: Turbo recommends Da-Lite easel #43145. Order from Mike Boer at Slide & Sound Corporation, (503) 615-0402.

↤↦

Ask Team Members What They Need

Tony, team leader for an equipment manufacturer, discovers that brainstorming is a great way to ask:

"For some time, my team members and I had wanted to have more training in our area. I knew we really wanted and needed meaningful training. I was hesitant to seek out a single training company because I thought that everyone on the team would want something different. One thing was for sure: the first thing I had to do was find out where to start.

"I made a decision to have a brainstorming session with everyone in our department. Because we are a small group, I knew I needed the complete involvement of everyone or the effort would fall on its face. I titled our session, simply, "Training Goals and Needs." The purpose of the brainstorming session was to get our group to commit to some training and improvement goals.

"I assured them that each person's ideas were valuable; all would be discussed openly. I told them one of the rules of brainstorming is that no one would criticize or condemn others' ideas, and no complaining would occur.

"We started out tentatively. A few suggestions were put forward. As soon as everyone saw that no one would throw cold water on their ideas or make personal attacks, they began to open up and the ideas started to flow.

"Because every idea has merit, I guaranteed that everyone's suggestions would be written down. I was writing as fast as the ideas came. Each idea built on the idea before it (a concept known as hitchhiking or synergy). When we were finally done, everyone had contributed at least three training goals and numerous ideas on how I could back them up.

⤷ *"The lesson I learned from this experience is, as the old* saying goes, 'You'll never find out unless you ask.' A well-run brainstorming meeting is a great way to ask."

"Put It in the Can"

Before you begin your brainstorming session, put a positive spin on your issues. Phrase your situation or problem as a question. Put it "in the can." In what ways can we: reduce costs...reduce time of work in progress...increase sales...operate more safely? Keep in mind the following:

Nine Rules for Brainstorming

- ↳ Go for quantity, not quality
- ↳ Encourage free thinking
- ↳ Green-light thinking only
- ↳ Everyone is encouraged to participate
- ↳ Write down everyone's ideas
- ↳ Encourage humor
- ↳ No personal criticism, put-down or judgment
- ↳ Always use a flip chart
- ↳ Keep the meeting moving by setting time limits

TOWARD BETTER MEETINGS

Ground Rules for Meetings

One of the best ways to improve the quality of your meetings is to reach an agreement about acceptable and unacceptable meeting behavior. We call this a "Code of Conduct." When these agreements have been reached, have your 6 to 12 code of conduct rules printed up and placed on the wall where everyone can see them. If anyone breaks one of the rules, just point to the rule being broken. This will help your meeting run at a much higher level. Here are some suggestions:

☑ Cell phones off

☑ Be open-minded, remain positive

☑ Make no personal attacks

☑ Don't interrupt; listen. No side conversations

☑ No gossip; facts only

☑ Complete the past—don't let history color today

☑ Honestly say what's on your mind, speak truthfully

☑ Lighten up, have fun

☑ If you don't understand, stop and ask

☑ Ask for and make energetic commitments

☑ Appreciate. When you see good things happening, say so!

☑ Support team decisions; speak with one voice afterwards

⇤⇥

MEETING PROCESS EVALUATION

Keeping Score: The Meeting Scorecard

Another tool you can use to improve the quality of your

meetings is a meeting scorecard. This is an excellent way to stimulate high-level team participation and make these professional practices a reality in your organization

At the end of your meeting, ask everyone to evaluate the session in these six areas:

☐Listening   ☐Decision Making

☐Participation   ☐Committing

☐Respect   ☐Light touch—sense of humor

Use this activity as a basis for analysis and discussion.

Team Process Check: Relative Rating						
Listening	10	9	8	7	6	5
Participation	10	9	8	7	6	5
Respect	10	9	8	7	6	5
Decision-making	10	9	8	7	6	5
Committing	10	9	8	7	6	5
Light touch	10	9	8	7	6	5

Suggestions for discussion:

↻ If everyone tends to agree, and scores are high, congratulate the team.

↻ If everyone tends to agree, and scores are low, ask the team what can be done to improve.

↻ If several people rated a category in a high range, and only one rated it low, explore why one person might have a quite different experience from the rest of the team.

My Meeting Critique

You will do yourself a great favor if, after your meeting, you take additional steps to evaluate the session, either on your own or with a coach. The following are some good questions you can use for critiquing and evaluating your meetings:

- ↻ Did we fulfill the overall purpose?
- ↻ What did I do well?
- ↻ What will I do differently next time?
- ↻ What challenges were presented?
- ↻ What did I do to meet the challenges?
- ↻ If need be, where might I secure assistance (aid, cooperation, training, guidance etc.)?
- ↻ Did we re-plow old ground?
- ↻ Did we start and stop on time?

Planning My Next Meeting

It's useful to have a tool, a simple form you can use in planning your meetings. The following are some ideas of what you might include on such a form:

Overall Purpose:

Specific Meeting Objectives: (What I want to accomplish)

What I need:

Opening: (The high point of the month for me)

Points I will make:

Anticipated problems, barriers or objections? I will Overcome them by:

Inspiration and call to action:

SUMMARY

Actions for Empowering Leaders:

- ↻ Plan the length and frequency of your meetings
- ↻ Buy a sturdy easel with pad for your meetings
- ↻ Tap the creativity of your team by brainstorming "In what ways can we…?"
- ↻ Publish goals and report your team's accomplishments
- ↻ Ask for a thoughtful critique of your meetings

Benefits You Will Gain:

- ↻ You will have a motivated team that works together to solve problems
- ↻ Your team will look forward to your meetings
- ↻ Your meetings will be productive
- ↻ You will solve your communication problems
- ↻ Your team will have renewed respect for you

Chapter Seven

ASKING THE RIGHT QUESTIONS

ASKING QUESTIONS EFFECTIVELY

A Sunday school teacher asked her class, "How many of you children want to go to heaven?" Everybody raised their hand but little Johnny. The teacher asked, "Johnny, don't you want to go to heaven when you die?" "Oh, when I die, yes!" exclaimed Johnny, "I thought you were getting a busload together right now."

Asking the right questions does not give an impression of ignorance or weakness. Others' respect for you grows steadily when you show, by asking, that you are interested in, and value, their ideas. Our surveys with thousands of front-line associates indicate that less than 25% of managers effectively determine the needs of associates who must support their decisions. Start asking questions effectively and others will open up to tell you what they think.

Through the process, you will gain great ideas, get their support and earn your team's heartfelt engagement.

THE ART OF CONVERSATION

Early in my career I sold office machines. I lacked a lot of confidence; I was comfortable as long as I was talking about the typewriters, computers, and copy machines I sold. When demonstrating the equipment, I knew the features and related benefits. I knew how to talk about those benefits so prospects could see how my products could help them resolve a problem or get better results.

But if a customer suggested going to lunch, I was petrified. Why? Because I had no idea what to talk about at lunch! And, I'm probably not the only person who has been uncomfortable with an invitation to the wedding of one of my wife's distant relatives. Luckily, I learned a secret for turning these fears into poise and confidence.

> ≳ *Getting to know someone is not a task—it's an art.* ≴
> - Pierce LeBlanc

I call it the "art of conversation." The art of conversation is the skillful use of a few questions. A good conversationalist has developed the ability to ask questions and to be attentive to the answers they hear. By perfecting the art and skill of asking well-worded questions, you can direct the conversation to give others an opportunity to express themselves. With well-worded questions, you will be comfortable and in charge. You take your conversational ability to a level that causes others to see you as a poised professional.

Now, when I meet someone at a wedding reception, a business luncheon, at church, on airplanes, anytime I meet people for the first time, I use these questions:

I introduce myself by saying, "My name is Larry." (*Pause... implied question, "What's yours?"*) If it makes sense, "We live out here in Newberg;" or "We live over on Wilsonville Road;" or "We live in Oregon. Do you live in the area?"

If it seems appropriate, I lead off by telling them about my family, and then ask about theirs.

"What kind of work do you do?"

"How long have you been doing that kind of work?"

"That sounds interesting. What do you enjoy most about it?"

"What's the most difficult or challenging part of your job, being in your business these days?"

I ask about the occasion. If I'm on an airplane, "What are you going to be doing in Toronto (town we are traveling to)?" or, "What do you think about the new hospital we're building in Newberg?"

"Who brought you to church today? What did they tell you about us that made you decide you wanted to visit?"

⇤⇥

THE QUESTION THAT NEVER FAILS

To become a great conversationalist, get clarification by asking pointed questions. Don't ever make the mistake of assuming you understand what a person is trying to say.

"How do you mean, exactly?"

To enliven the conversation and put yourself in control, suggests my friend Brian, try this simple question: *How do you mean, exactly?* It's amazing—it never fails. The other person finds it almost impossible not to answer in detail. You can follow up with more open-ended questions to keep the conversation rolling along. This is the art of conversation.

↹

PUT QUESTION POWER TO WORK FOR YOU

Worded correctly, questions do more than get answers. They get results—by spurring associates to action, building consensus and clearing up confusion. Poorly worded questions, on the other hand, block idea exchange, sap enthusiasm and can even foster resentment.

As an empowering leader, to have an accurate picture, to evaluate results, to improve job performance, you must know all the facts, including what motivates and inspires your associates. Asking the right questions in the right way will help. Your well-worded, carefully considered questions will draw attention to what you value, and help your associates think more precisely. Knowing that you will ask these questions draws their attention to what they need to know, and adds direction to their efforts and improvement to their performance.

Why do we sometimes neglect to ask questions? Failing to ask the right questions can waste time, and cause embarrassment, frustration and lost profits. What questions have you used that have given you a clear idea of what you need to do, helped you save time, money or frustration? What questions do you need to use more often to improve your performance and effectiveness?

↹

In The Elephants' Child, Rudyard Kipling puts it this way:

> *"I keep six honest serving men*
> *(They taught me all I knew);*
> *Their names are What and Why and When*
> *and How and Where*
> *and Who."*

You will be successful and confident as you develop your ability to demonstrate interest in others by asking these and other related questions.

THE QUESTION IN QUESTION

A question is defined as the interrogation by which information is secured. There are two kinds of questions: Fact-Finding Questions and Feeling Finding Questions. Let's compare the two:

> ⋟ *A man is like an island... you want to row around it a couple of times before you decide where to land.* ⋞

Fact-Finding Questions

Fact-finding questions help you gather the information you need to analyze, solve problems, make decisions and execute those decisions in the timeliest manner possible. Fact finding questions target the facts.

In the old TV series, "Dragnet," Joe Friday's famous hallmark line was "Just the facts, ma'am." Be "sleuthful," not slothful. Always find out when it is needed, where it is needed, who needs it, how it is to be used and, most importantly, what results you are accountable for. Get to the reason behind the action—the why behind the what.

"Your Place or Mine?"

Don, staff manager for an equipment manufacturer, forgot to ask an important question:

"Early in my career, I went to work for a manufacturer in Cincinnati. After a few years, I earned my first promotion to a management position. Along with the promotion and appointment to manager came a move to the company's plant in Indiana.

"My new plant was located about one-and-a half hours from the Corporate Office in Cincinnati. It was within easy driving distance for visits back and forth the same day. My boss, the Vice President of Manufacturing, came to my plant in Indiana for a day's visit with me on most Wednesdays.

"One Monday morning, my boss called and asked if I could be in the office the next day. Of course I said I could. He declared the time of our meeting to be 9:00 AM and we proceeded briefly outlining verbally the subject we would cover in detail the following day.

"As a young up-and-coming manager, I certainly wanted to make a good impression on my visit to the Corporate Office, so I left with plenty of time to spare to assure that I would not be late. I dressed carefully for the occasion— blue suit, heavily starched and pressed white shirt, red tie, black wing tipped shoes and a new leather briefcase carrying every possible detail of the subject. I was as well prepared as a criminal lawyer—John T. Molloy of *Dress for Success* would have been proud.

"I arrived a few minutes early and went directly to my

boss' office. The lights were out so I went across the hall to the canteen for a cup of coffee. I then went to the secretary's office and asked if Mr. Ionna had arrived. She responded, 'Well, no. He went to your Indiana plant early this morning to visit you!'

↳ *"The lesson I learned from this experience is to ask the right follow-up questions and listen well to everything being said. If I had simply clarified, 'Your office or my office?', I would have met with Mr. Ionna that Tuesday morning, and saved a lot of embarrassment and explaining. Even though I had so diligently prepared, prepared I was not."*

↤↴

Getting to the Basics with Fact-Finding Questions

Fact-finding questions usually start with *What, When, Where, Who,* or *How.*

These are questions to ask about assignments you are given, or questions to answer when making assignments:

- ↻ "What are we going to do?" (details of an assignment or project)
- ↻ "When do we start?" (schedule)
- ↻ "Where does it fit in?" (priority)
- ↻ "When is it needed?" (how long do we have?)
- ↻ "How do we proceed?" (plan or approach)
- ↻ "Why are we doing it?" (provides context)
- ↻ "Who is going to do it?" (staff and personnel)
- ↻ "What are the benefits?" (purpose)

Here are some examples of fact-finding questions:

↻What? What is the first thing you cover in your meetings?

What are you looking for in a new employee?

What is the first thing you cover in your meetings?

What was decided about the new computers?

What did you compliment her on?"

↻When? When did you meet?

When did you update these charts?

When will we implement this plan?

When do you tell them you appreciated their staying late?

↻Where? Where will the meeting be held?

Where do you post performance charts?

Where can your supervisors find the safety reports?

↻Who? Who is in charge of _____?

Who is responsible for finishing this job?

Who will take notes in the meeting?

↻How? How did you do that?

How does this work?

How are new office procedures handled?

Note: Some fact-finding questions require a yes or no response:

↻Yes or No? Is there a formal annual review?

Do you use a professional service to check applicants' credit ratings?

Do you offer a matching 401-K plan?

↹

What Disqualifies a Fact-Finding Question?

It is important that you learn to distinguish between fact-finding and feeling-finding questions. Fact-finding questions are NOT open-ended. They are never leading or biased. Fact-finding questions never start with "Do you think…?" "How do you think…? "Do you feel…? "How do you feel about…?" The answers are tainted by that person's point of view or personal perspective.

If you are asking these questions, you are asking feeling-finding questions.

⇤

FEELING-FINDING QUESTIONS

Asking feeling-finding questions in the right way elicits an accurate understanding, a clear picture of how your associates see things, how they feel about things—any and all opinions and emotions that are relevant.

Feeling-finding questions help you gain a window into another person's perspective, viewpoint and feelings. They enable you to learn about your associates' opinions, aspirations and desires, and help you discover what motivates and inspires them. When properly used, feeling-finding questions help you see the world through your associate's lens.

Most effective feeling-finding questions are open-ended. Open-ended questions cannot be answered with a simple "yes" or "no." Open-ended questions encourage the speaker to expand on their thoughts and comments. One question will lead to another. You can ask open-ended, wide-angle questions almost endlessly, drawing out everything the other person has to say on a particular subject.

⇤

Open-Ended Questioning Pays Off

Steve, swing-shift supervisor for a machine shop, asks that magic open-ended question:

"Last May, I hired a young man to work in our machine shop. Ten months have passed and he has turned out to be an excellent crew member in every respect. I love having him on my team. In spite of this, as I made my way around the shop every night, practicing 'Shoe-Leather Leadership' (see Chapter Nine), to talk with every associate on the floor, I felt a sense of dread as I approached his work station. This seems very strange, considering what a great worker he is. The problem was we just couldn't seem to hold a conversation. Our conversational skills were very similar; that is to say, not too good. We would smile, and be polite, but words were often replaced by extremely awkward moments of silence and staring at one another.

"About three weeks ago, I chose this person to be my 'Person Pearl.' I felt he had a great deal of potential and I wanted to improve our relationship. I looked through the 15 Leadership Principles, and decided I would focus on #2: Become Genuinely Interested. One afternoon, as I approached his work station I commented on how quickly he had learned to set up and run a very complex machine.

Then I asked the magic open-ended question, 'How did you do that?' His eyes lit up. He explained in some detail about how a recent programming class he had taken had helped him really understand the complexities of the machine.

"We then talked about other classes he was taking. It worked! We finally had a conversation that we both enjoyed and felt comfortable with. I made it a point to go back to his area two or three times a day, with open ended questions. Overall, our relationship is greatly improved. He surprised me yesterday by telling me about a personal situation going on within his household. It felt to me like he, too, was trying to improve our relationship. I know that this conversation would not have taken place four weeks ago.

↳ *"The lesson I learned from this experience is that I am able to build relationships by asking open-ended questions. I learned that open-ended questions may be one of the best ways to show appreciation and demonstrate a genuine interest."*

When you ask open-ended questions you are giving associates a chance to talk about their favorite subject: themselves, their interests, their opinions.

Helpful Feeling-Finding Questions:

- ↺ For feeling-finding questions to elicit true feelings, they must be asked in neutral tones. You may wish to emphasize certain words:
- ↺ "How do you feel about...?"
- ↺ "What is your opinion...?"
- ↺ "What would you suggest...?"
- ↺ "Why is that important to you...?"
- ↺ "What do you think the real problem is?"
- ↺ "What do you think you need to get the job done?"
- ↺ "Would it be fair to ask what you like least about...?"
- ↺ "Do you think it would be better if...?"
  (Be careful! This could be a leading question!)

Ask, Ask, and Keep On Asking

Dick, crew foreman of an earth-moving construction company, asks and keeps on asking:

"One of my operators had been very reluctant to contribute any of his ideas on how to solve the many operating problems we were having on one of our recent complex jobs. He wanted me to be the one to come up with all the innovative suggestions and ideas to bring the job in on schedule and under budget.

"Returning to work after being delayed and set back by bad, rainy weather, we were confronted with a lot of muddy, soft ground. We were behind schedule as it was, and late charges were looming over our heads. We were in trouble!

"I called the operator aside and more or less pleaded with him for some advice. I said, 'I don't know what to do. You have seen situations like this before. What has worked in the past for you?'

"I encouraged, implored and honestly said, 'I don't know how to do it--and I know you do.' I finally opened up a space by listening with silence and he cautiously began to tell me his ideas. I listened carefully to his advice, we tried his suggestions, and shazzam, it worked! We began to make up some of our lost time. I thanked him profusely for his advice and praised him for helping solve the seemingly hopeless problem. Profusely praising the successes we enjoyed by using his ideas seems to have opened up a reservoir. He is now much more willing to contribute to our team effort.

⤷ *"The lesson I have learned from this experience is that it pays to persist in asking the right questions. When I honestly look for and use the ideas of my crew, performance significantly improves."*

⇤⇥

Broaden the Scope of Your Questions

Here are more useful questions:

Wide-Angle Follow-Up Questions

To draw out your listener, follow up with *wide-angle questions* such as these:

- ↻ "Why do you think that would be important?"
- ↻ "Could you tell me more about that?"
- ↻ "Could you give me another example?
- ↻ "Where will it go next?"
- ↻ "How will this work?"
- ↻ "How would this work?"

Direct questions

…encourage others to share opinions and take ownership of a problem:

- ↻ "How can we complete this project on time?" This question directs the associate to a solution, not a description of the problem.

"Planted-answer" questions

… imply the specific direction you want your associate's answer to take. Use them to gain "buy-in:"

- ↻ "Do you agree this outline needs more work?"(Don't overdo this kind of question. Your associates can see through them—you are really saying that the outline needs more work. Why not be more honest, more direct?)

"Off the hook" questions:

...allow associates to refuse without losing face. Use them to signal that they have a choice:

- ↻ "I know you've already put in a lot of overtime this week. Would it be possible for you to stay a little late again tonight?" (Don't ask this question if you can't live with a "no.")

↻

Questions to Stimulate Creativity

Most managers tend to feel they should have all the answers. Your long-term success is far more likely to stem from the answers you receive to your well-worded questions. Here are some guidelines:

- ↻ Use questions to encourage innovation. Instead of "Have that to me by Friday," ask, "What has to happen for you to complete this by Friday?"
- ↻ Replace "I put the printouts on your desk" with, "Do you have all the information you need?"
- ↻ Rather than "I have some questions about the marketing numbers you came up with," ask, "What part of the report would you like to talk about in depth?"

Avoid morale-sapping questions:

- ↻ Disagreeable questions that reduce self-confidence. They are seen as an attack: "None of your other ideas have worked out. What makes you think this one will?"
- ↻ "No-way-out" questions that drive your associates

into corners and encourage defensive responses: "As I see it, this is the only solution. How can you possibly disagree?"

↻ Trick questions that are traps to get others to agree with you because they're left with little or no choice: "Should we follow my plan as it is, or put in some long hours to revamp it?"

Don't use weak questions that go nowhere:

↻ "What's new today, Bill?"

↻ "Do you like your work, Mary?"

↻ "Did you have a good day today, Jim?"

↹

THE "INNER-VIEW"

One of the best ways to create understanding, build rapport, and eliminate communication barriers is to conduct an "inner-view" of key associates. "Inner-viewing" is a way for you to look deeper than the surface, to find out what makes your associates "tick." Begin by getting more deeply involved in what they are doing. Demonstrate genuine interest; make it your goal to know and understand what they think and feel about themselves and about their jobs. You will earn their trust, and they will perform at a higher level.

↹

"Inner-View" Demonstrates Genuine Interest

Here's a great story! How inner-viewing helped John, plant manager for a tube forging company, become better acquainted with his associates:

"I guess I had known for some time that I needed to become more involved with our production associates out in the plant. The feedback from our Leadership Team Advance made the point even more obvious. I needed to demonstrate a genuine interest and concern. I needed to listen and learn in order to become the positive, empowered leader the team deserves.

"I decided to put together an action plan. I started with Shoe-Leather Leadership (see Chapter Nine, Acknowledgment), going out on the floor for 15 to 20 minutes every day. My plan was designed to ensure that over a period of time I would have continual successful encounters with our entire team. Through this process, I would really be aware of their world. This action plan was helpful; in only a few days I was better informed about what was going on, but I was still not completely satisfied with the results. The real one-on-one quality time I needed with our frontline team could not happen with only these brief visits through the plant.

"The second step in my action plan was to start coming in on Saturdays to spend two or three hours working on various lines with our crew members. I did this in many areas of the plant, including cutting, welding, tube forging, etc.

"Through these efforts, I began to develop the personal relationships that had been missing. Communication has grown and improved dramatically. I have gotten to know our associates better and I can tell they are beginning to feel they know me. We have all enjoyed our time together. What they really enjoy is seeing me get dirty as we work together. Their hardships have now become my hardships and their difficulties and problems have also become mine.

Real understanding and learning has taken place. I am thrilled. I have never felt so good about working at this company. I have begun to really feel that I have been accepted by the crew!

↳ *"The lesson I learned is that one-on-one communication with all team members is extremely important. I have learned that reports may help, but for the team to really be in formation, I need one-on-one information."*

Examples of "Inner-View" Questions

- ↻ You might start by saying: "What I know about you is . . ." (briefly summarize.) "I'd like to know you a little better. Would it be OK if I ask you a few questions?"
- ↻ Tell me a little about your early life.
- ↻ What activities were you involved in high school?
- ↻ If you could start over again, what would you do differently?
- ↻ What do you do for recreation and fun?
- ↻ What is your idea of a great vacation?
- ↻ What do you find most stimulating and challenging about your work?
- ↻ Are there some things you don't like about your work? What is most difficult? (Of course, we all know there are things we do not like about any job.)
- ↻ What skills and abilities do you believe you have that enable you to perform your job well?
- ↻ What gives you the greatest gratification in your present position?
- ↻ What would you like to be doing in five or ten years?

- ↻ What are some of your personal goals in life, short and long-range?
- ↻ Are your goals in your head, or do you have them written down?
- ↻ Who has had the most profound effect upon your life? How? Who are some others who had an influence on you? How?
- ↻ For management position interviews:
- ↻ What do you like best about being a manager?
- ↻ What qualities do you look for when interviewing an applicant?
- ↻ What qualities do you look for when promoting an associate?
- ↻ What do you feel are the most important leadership skills you must have in your position?
- ↻ What do you feel has been your most important contribution so far to our industry?
- ↻ If a young person came to you for advice just before going out into the world, what advice would you give them?

Finally:

Remember that questioning is a two-way, ↳*Feedforward*/feedback↻ street!

Encourage your staff to ask questions of you. Share your vision and values, your enthusiasm, your highest expectations. You'll stimulate them to think more about your business and their roles, and about possible improvements.

⇆

SUMMARY

Actions for Empowering Leaders

- ↻ Practice asking pure fact-finding questions to get more, better ideas
- ↻ Ask feeling-finding questions to strengthen understanding
- ↻ Ask questions to understand why
- ↻ Request information with open-minded inquiries
- ↻ Ask questions to get more and better ideas

Benefits You Will Gain:

- ↻ You will be more organized and productive
- ↻ Your communication will significantly improve
- ↻ You will be a positive, empowering leader
- ↻ You will be armed with new ideas
- ↻ Your associates will be aware of their role in your business

Chapter Eight

LISTENING

CONSCIOUS LISTENING

Communication is much more than sending a message. At least 50% of all effective communication is listening. Most people seem to feel they listen well, especially those who don't. Effective listening skills are as important for an empowering leader as effective speaking skills. We were created with one tongue and two ears. Empowering leaders use them proportionately.

Good communicators are competent receivers. Think about your best friends. One probable reason they rank as "best" friends is that they are good listeners. We must be skilled observers—aware of all the feedback, both verbal and nonverbal, that comes our way.

We have a deep, almost primal need to be heard. Feeling we have been heard means that not only have we been listened to, we've been understood. When we, as empowering leaders, provide listening that causes our associates to feel they have been heard, we satisfy one of their deepest needs. There is something within this kind of listening that causes us to feel believed in, and empowers us to perform beyond our former levels of engagement.

Seven out of every ten minutes that we are conscious, alive and awake, we are sending or receiving communication. Effective communication time falls into the following categories:

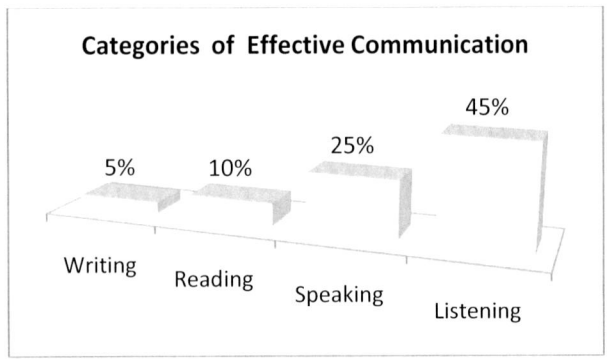

The next time an associate is trying to tell you about their problem, don't be too quick to give an answer, ask for a solution or point them in the right direction. First, let them know you hear how they feel. This alignment of feelings will in fact improve the harmony of your relationship. Feeling with empathy will create a marriage of your minds. This will help you pull in the same direction, and create synergism, one of the secrets of improving results.

An important difference

Are you listening, or are you just waiting for your turn to talk? When you think you know what's coming, are you already preparing your response? Empowering leaders first listen fully to what's really being

> ⋛ *No one has a better command of language than the man who keeps his mouth shut.* ⋛
> Sam Ravburn

communicated, and only then formulate what they want to say.

↹

Listening Ranks High

A leading university recently spent 18 months trying to determine the attributes of a good leader. The study came up with this generalization:

> *Of all the sources of information by which leaders can come to know and accurately size up the personalities of the people in their departments, listening is the most important.*

In trying to make a profile of a good leader, the most typical report from worker after worker was this: "I like my boss because she listens to me. I can talk to her."

As stated by the American Management Association School of Management, "Efficient listening is of such critical importance in industry that as research and methodology improve, training departments will have to offer courses specifically to increase our listening ability."

↹

"All I Did Was Listen!"

Debra, office manager for an over-the-highway trucking company, "bit her tongue and listened:"

"My 13-year old daughter walked into my bedroom the other evening and said, 'I need to talk with you, Mom.' I could tell immediately that something was up. After hemming and hawing for a few minutes, she finally told me she and her 16-year old boyfriend were thinking about having sex!

"At that point, I exercised more self-restraint than ever before in my life. I wanted to say a lot of things: AIDS! Pregnancy! Is that all I have taught you? Instead, I applied Leadership Principle #6 - *Be an Active Listener*. I bit my tongue and let her talk it out without interrupting. When she started to run down, I encouraged her to tell me all she could about her feelings.

"Finally, after about an hour, with me silently listening most of the time, Merissa ended up stating, with great resolve, that she had decided she was going to follow my advice. What advice? I pondered. All I did was listen and then tell her a story about a friend of mine from high school.

"'I am not going to have sex until I'm married,' Merissa said. If her boyfriend didn't understand, then he was not the right guy for her. Again, I restrained myself, trying not to preach. Instead, I congratulated her on her insight and resolve, and the conclusion she had arrived at on her own.

↳ *"The lesson I learned is that if I bite my tongue, hold back my tendency to preach, and resist knee-jerk reactions; if I wait for the other person to finish talking out their feelings and reasoning out their ideas, I have extraordinary influence!"*

LISTENING TO MAKE A DIFFERENCE

LISTENING
That Makes No Positive Difference

NON-HEARING	**TAPE-RECORDER**	**EMPATHETIC**
Can include eye contact, head-shaking, saying "uh-huh." Listener is thinking about something else or waiting for his turn to talk and does not even hear what is said.	Listener provides the courtesy of hearing the words and can repeat them back, but was not really there for the communication.	Hears the speaker and has compassion for the speaker, but nothing is altered as a result of the communication.

LISTENING
With the Intention to Make a Difference

Subject: **What's Working?**	Subject: **What's Not Working?**
• Acknowledge or praise the appropriate person's actions. • Describe the positive impact of what happened. • Challenge the speaker to take on the next action project.	• Direct the speaker to do something to correct the situation. • Direct the speaker to someone who can help to correct the situation. • Offer support regarding the resolution of the situation.
Results in a Feeling of Accomplishment and Further Positive Action	Results in Commitment to Corrective Action

MAXIMIZE LISTENING SKILLS

Listening skills aren't easy to master. With practice and patience, you can become an excellent listener.

When you maximize your listening skills, hearing beyond words and understanding the feelings beneath the words, you protect and nourish successful relationships. Here's how to get the most out of your listening skills:

"Lend Me Your Ear"

- Develop an inquiring mind. You can find areas of interest in most messages. Be receptive; look for ways to use the information. This builds tolerance and patience into listening.

- Focus on the key concepts of what you are hearing; identify the speaker's main points. Be a concept listener rather than a fact listener.

- Pay total attention, keeping your mind on the speaker, not on framing your response. Resist the temptation to mentally debate rather than listen.

- Hold your fire—Make sure you understand the message before judging. It is wise to slow down the listening process. Ask questions to check your understanding before agreeing or disagreeing with the information.

- Paraphrase the speaker's words. When you say, "Let me see if I've got this right. What you're saying is...,"(restating in your own words), you demonstrate that you are genuinely paying attention and making every effort to understand their thoughts and feelings.

- Listen "between the lines" to the tone of voice for clues to what's not necessarily put into words, to see if there's something that wasn't said. Ask yourself, "Is the speaker purposely skirting some subject? Why?"

- Pay attention to body language. Notice the speaker's facial expressions, posture and gestures that add meaning to their message. Observe as well as listen.

- Keep your attention focused; you are able to think much faster than the speaker can speak. Use thought speed to mentally summarize information, and listen for deeper meanings.

- Pause three to five seconds before replying to show that you are giving careful consideration to their words. This allows time for their words to reach a deeper level in your mind, and you will understand with greater clarity.

Seven Keys to Effective Listening

So, with the above in mind, here are more perceptive ways to improve your listening skills. These keys are positive guidelines to better listening. In fact, they are at the heart of developing better listening habits that could serve you for a lifetime:

Key 🔑	The Poor Listener: ☹	The Good Listener: ☺
Find areas of interest	*Tunes out dry subjects*	Asks, "What's in it for me?"
Judge content, not delivery	*Tunes out if delivery is poor*	Judges content, skips over delivery errors
Listen for ideas	*Listens for facts alone*	Listens for central themes
Be flexible	*Concentrates on taking extensive notes*	Takes only key notes
Exercise your mind	*Resists difficult material, seeks easy material*	Challenges mind with unfamiliar material
Keep your mind open	*Reacts to emotional words*	Does not get hung up on emotional words
Capitalize on the fact that thought is faster than speech	*Tends to daydream with slow speakers*	Mentally summarizes, and listens for deeper meaning

Effective Listening Pays Off

Alan effectively used the Seven Keys:

"In conversation with one of my managers, I was tipped off that Carleen may have felt I was treating her differently from others in our office. With this in mind, I made a point to be proactive and initiate a conversation with her the next day. Knowing that it would be hard work and take me out of my comfort zone, I planned to force myself to really listen to her point of view without judgment.

"I followed Turbo's Seven Keys to Effective Listening; I urged Carleen to be honest and express her feelings. She came back to me the following day to tell me how much better she felt and how much she appreciated my attention.

"I have resolved to always be available and receptive to my associates, to really listen to what they say, not waste time justifying, excusing or telling them why they are wrong.

↳*"The lesson I learned from this experience is that by listening and being attentive to my entire team, I am facilitating genuine, meaningful understanding and communication."*

↹

Listening Empowers Associate

Gary, buyer for an equipment manufacturer, provides leadership by listening intently:

"Several weeks ago, I was approached in the warehouse by one of our associates. I was somewhat surprised by the question she asked me, 'Do you think I do a good job?' By her expression, I concluded she was feeling hurt. I followed up her question with a question of my own, 'Why would you ask a question like that?'

"This gave her the opening she was looking for. She told me she was hurt because she had overheard two of her co-workers talking about her. They felt she was not pulling her weight any longer. I answered her question by telling her I thought she was doing a great job. I asked her if she had an idea why anyone would think or feel otherwise. She said she had recently been very busy, and unable to help other departments out like she had in the past.

"I suggested she look for an opening to explain to her co-workers what was going on in her own work area that kept her from being able to help them out, and tell them she hoped to be able to be more available again in the near future.

"Several hours later, I ran into her again. I could see immediately that she was in a much better mood. I asked her if she had been able to have her little talk. She replied that she had initiated a conversation with the co-workers and told them about her expanded workload. They had easily worked out their differences.

↳ *"The lesson I learned from this experience is that by being willing and able to listen to team members, I can provide the leadership that is needed to reinforce their self-worth. Sometimes I can even help them work out their differences with others."*

What I love about this story is that Gary didn't condemn the other parties involved. And, he didn't let the monkey get on his back by saying, "Let me see what I can do about that." Instead, he listened very carefully. After listening, he was able to give a couple of simple suggestions that empowered his team members.

↰↳

Listening Revitalizes Relationship

Bob, president of a major Portland area contracting firm, stops and listens:

"The past couple of years, it seems like Cece, my wife of 34 years, and I have been bickering about anything and everything. Between her mood swings and my tuning her out most of the time, life at home was getting very difficult. I now realize that because I was not 100% committed to our marriage, our relationship wasn't good for either one of us.

"In Session 2 of the Leadership Lab, I chose Cece as one of my 'Person Pearl' as part of a class assignment. I committed to use Leadership Principle #6 - *Be an Active Listener* to demonstrate my increased commitment and improve our relationship.

"After three weeks of my practicing the active listening principle by stopping whatever I was doing any time Cece wanted to talk, and really listening to Cece's thoughts and ideas. Our situation at home improved dramatically! In fact, at the end of the fourth week, we were just relaxing in front of the television when Cece commented that we had not had a single argument all week. She went on to say she felt a meaningful, positive change in our relationship. It was true the bickering had subsided because I had made a conscious effort to LISTEN. Unconsciously, I had begun to use another of the 15 Leadership Principles, #5 - *See Their*

Point of View. I was trying honestly to see her point of view.

↳ *"The lesson I learned from this experience is when I really listen, I not only learn, I empower change in other people without them even realizing it."*

⇥

When Bob invited me to have lunch with him and his wife Cece, she said, "I wanted to meet the man who's changed my husband." "Did you say, *changed* your husband?" I asked. She replied, "Yes, changed my husband!"

"I don't believe it. Give me proof that he's changed," I said. She went on to tell me about working together on their Jeep. They both are dedicated to one of their hobbies, off-road 4-wheeling. She described Bob lying under the Jeep *asking, not ordering,* her to hand him parts and wrenches, with an entirely new approach, very different from the demanding style of the past.

"Enough." I said. "You've proven it to me. Bob is a changed man."

What's my point? My point is this; "I can't change" may be a convenient excuse for not putting forth the effort, undergoing the pain, the fear, the uneasiness that occurs with all significant change. If you want to change, it is possible. If Bob and Cece can reinvent their relationship after 34 years, I'm confident that you too can reinvent your relationships—with your boss, your subordinates, your coordinates, your children and even your spouse.

⇥

{{A-C-T-I-V-E}} LISTENING

{{A}}-**Attentive Attitude**—Free your mind of distracting thoughts. Develop powers of concentration. Learn to ignore distractions. Good listeners seem to be able to will themselves into listening. The more you work at concentrating while listening, the more your power of concentration develops and the easier listening becomes. Do not yawn.

{{C}}-**Comfortable Environment**—Be in the right situation with associates. Actively reduce controllable noise by closing doors and holding calls. Clear your mind. Sometimes it is useful to clear your desk or put down your papers.

{{T}}-**Take Time**—Put other things aside. Make the associate the center of importance. Give your complete attention. Let them know you are listening. Maintain constant eye contact; nod your head. Ninety-eight percent of all that people learn over their lifetimes is learned through their eyes and ears. Restate their main points to check understanding and invite feedback. That way, misunderstanding or faulty assumptions can be discovered early and corrected.

{{I}}-**Investigate**—Ask searching questions. Ask about their statements. Dig out information. Invite them to tell everything. Say, "In addition to that, is there anything else?" Paraphrase their remarks. Keep the conversation in your mind. Remain neutral. Do not give advice, agree, disagree, criticize or interrupt. Put judgments on hold.

{{V}}-**Verbal/Non-Verbal Response**—Nod; smile; keep good eye contact. Communicators who are hurt often make a costly mistake—we forget to look each other straight in the eye, thereby missing important nonverbal cues. Hurt, anger, fear and sadness come out subconsciously in small gestures. For example, a speaker may be sounding tough, but feeling scared.

{{E}}-**Empathize**—Acknowledge their feelings. Put their feelings into words by paraphrasing what you heard and stating what their feelings seem to be. When they hear their feelings voiced by you, they may re-evaluate them. Summarize what you have both said; get agreement. Encourage the associate to suggest the next step or course of action.

Be as active when you listen as you are when you speak. Make the speaker feel important. You will get far more cooperation from people you listen to.

↹

Handling Conflict with Active Listening

- ↺ Paraphrase accurately and evaluate the content of the message from the sender
- ↺ Describe what you perceive to be the sender's feelings
- ↺ Check your interpretation of the sender's message
- ↺ Ask open-ended questions to explore the sender's thoughts, feelings and ideas
- ↺ State your own opinion in "I" terms
- ↺ Ask the associate to restate your point of view
- ↺ Let them know you are interested in reaching agreement
- ↺ "Three points of agreement, two points of negotiation, and one point of disagreement"

↹

Listening Increases Productivity

I recently met with Gerry, the general manager of a heavy truck manufacturing plant in our greater Portland area. They have over 1900 associates and they turn out 96 trucks a day. The company enjoys a 30% market share. The company has progressed over the past six years from taking 325 hours to build a truck to turning out a truck in only 125 hours. The new trucks are at least 25% more complex than the trucks they were building six years ago.

How have Gerry and his team done this? Of course there is

no simple answer. The Portland plant is the most productive plant of all six of the company's truck plants. They are unionized and have prescribed standards for the performance of every task that is performed within the manufacturing and assembly processes. The plant is running at 117% of standard, whereas some North American plants are as low as 82%. The non-unionized plants are running between 83% and 102%. Gerry is investing ten times more time in training all associates today than ever before. All jobs have standards for performance.

Gerry has nine taskforce teams throughout the plant. One taskforce team is made up of a cross-section of nine people in the plant who direct all other taskforce teams. The other teams are from the manufacturing floor; they devote an hour a week of overtime to problem-solving. They are sufficiently equipped and trained to draw up the standards for performance to create the necessary changes, achieve quality initiatives and eliminate warranty claims. They have a supervisor ratio of 175 people per supervisor. There is strict adherence to punctuality rules. Their people are paid 25% more per hour than many of the other truck plants, and still they are the most successful in terms of overall cost of production.

The plant has computer terminals at every location throughout the manufacturing process. These computer terminals allow workers to see how to perform their tasks. Since all their trucks are made to custom specifications it is essential that there is information readily available on how to make the modifications. Most of this plant is paperless so there is no work order following a truck through the plant, but rather a computer terminal which tells the assembler what to do on each particular project.

> ☑ **"My ideas make a difference in how things are done around here."**
> *(Cultural Benchmark Survey)*

If all of this sounds complex, it is. Gerry told me at the end of our second meeting, "If you want to increase productivity, the most important thing you can do as a manager is really listen to your fellow team members. If you listen to your people, you gain the benefit of their knowledge and you improve production and morale. If you don't listen to your people, you create problems.

"One of the smart things we do is to meet all new associates. The people whose names I know don't create problems; it's the ones whose names I don't know." As complex as his operation may be with standards, computers and reams of statistics, he still says the most important thing you can do is get to know and listen to your team members and treat them as if they are important.

⇄

SUMMARY

Actions for Empowering Leaders:

↻ Empower others by fully listening to them

↻ Acknowledge feelings as well as words

↻ Listen intently; don't plan your response at the same time

↻ Handle conflict with active listening

↻ Let the other person do the talking

The Benefits You Will Gain:

↻ You will increase the productivity of your team

↻ Your responses will be accurate and appropriate

↻ You will have more pleasurable teamwork

↻ Your associates will maintain a good attitude

↻ Your team will know they make a positive difference

Chapter Nine

ACKNOWLEDGMENT

EVERYONE APPRECIATES APPRECIATION

Do you like to get a compliment? A Japanese entrepreneur is betting you do. He offers on-the-spot flattery on the street corners of Tokyo—for a price of about a dollar a minute: "Great Armani jacket!" "What an unusual pair of eyes!"

We think that's pretty funny. But there's an important underlying truth here: Everyone appreciates being appreciated. Some are even willing to pay for it!

Your associates, too, appreciate in value, their contribution increases, when they feel appreciated. You can become a better "appreciator"—with practice.

A GAP IN PERCEPTION

On a scale of one to five, from "never" to "always," managers were asked to respond to the statement, "I let my team members know when they are doing a good job." Team members responded to a similar statement: "My supervisor lets me know when I am doing a good job." Same question, different perspective.

The managers rated themselves a 4.3. No surprise here—most managers think they do a great job of providing acknowledgment. The same managers were rated 2.3 by their subordinates. From the team's perspective, more than half the time they didn't receive the acknowledgment they felt they deserved. A huge gap in perception!

Why the big difference? Could it be the leaders didn't take the time or seek out opportunities to give positive feedback? Or perhaps they gave all their positive feedback to a few select employees? Could the reason be the employees in the survey weren't listening and were wrong in their assessment? The bottom line is, it doesn't matter who was right. Team members' perceptions are what counts, and their perceptions were that they were not receiving positive acknowledgment often enough.

> *Even though they are paid differently, everyone has the right to feel appreciated.*
> —Roger Staubach

MAINTAIN YOUR RELATIONSHIPS

We know that if we fail to maintain our cars, we'll eventually pay the price. Flashing lights on the dashboard help us remember to change the oil or add water to the radiator. We often excuse our lack of employee maintenance by saying: "They know they're doing a good job;" "If they weren't good at what they do, they wouldn't be here in the first place;" or "Joe knows he's good—why do I have to keep 'stroking?'" Managers who take that attitude are courting disaster. A leader who really works to maintain good interpersonal relationships learns to pay attention to how associates act, look and respond to acknowledgment.

Acknowledgment is an important way to earn the respect of your team, and at the same time, empower them. "We all want acknowledgment," Vance Packard said in *Hidden Persuaders*, "We have an itch we can't scratch." In other words, this is an unmet need, a need that is never completely satisfied. William James said **the deepest principle in human nature is the craving to be appreciated**. He didn't say we like it, need it or want it. He said we crave it.

↳↰

HITTING A HOME RUN WITH YOUR TEAM

"3 A's + a P"
The Baseball Diamond of Acknowledgment

Using the "**3 A's + a P**" acknowledgment process, empowering leaders hit a "home run" with their team. On this playing field, the first three bases are the **A's** of **A**cknowledgment: **A**ttention, **A**pproval, and **A**ppreciation; Home plate is the **P**: **P**raise.

First Base—the 'A' of Attention. You get to first base with your team and build rapport by **paying positive attention to team members**. How do team members earn your attention? *They show up.*

Second Base—the 'A' of Approval. You get to second base with your associates by **voicing your approval.** Team members earn approval by performing their jobs up to agreed-to standards.

Third Base—the 'A' of Appreciation. You get to third base by **showing appreciation.** Team members earn appreciation by going the extra mile, doing something beyond the call of duty.

Home Plate—the 'P' of Praise. You round the bases to home plate and win the game by **praising team members.** Focus on the quality of the individual that drives their behavior, and praise them for demonstrating that quality.

You advance one "base" at a time with everyone on your team. When you cover all the bases, you score. Your associates see themselves as more capable; they are growing in their roles and creatively giving their discretionary effort to the success of the enterprise.

As the team's contribution grows stronger, so does their respect and trust of you. And, just like the explosion of fireworks announcing a home run at the ball park, you too, experience excitement when you score a home run with your team!

1. FIRST BASE: PAYING ATTENTION

"Shoe-Leather Leadership©"

Empowering leaders actively demonstrate they care. They exercise *"Shoe-Leather Leadership"*—they get out from behind their desks. They visit every department. They know and acknowledge associates. Shoe-Leather Leadership takes place on the floor, in the field; it happens when you walk around. This is how you show you're paying attention to those who are on the frontline, in the trenches.

Most managers pay a lot of attention to people who fail to show up, and too often take for granted the ones they can rely on. Start the day with "Good morning. Glad to see you." Ask, "How did your son's hockey game turn out?" "How was your daughter's softball game?" Your associates want to know they are valued as more than an instrument of production; they want to know you take an interest in them, and they want to hear it from you.

Don't depend on technology to broadcast the message that you care. Trust can't be developed with memos, bulletins, and emails. A handshake and a look in the eye with a hearty "thank you" have far greater impact than any message on a computer screen.

These general guidelines will help ensure your Shoe-Leather Leadership visits are something everyone looks forward to:

Open with: "Good morning! Good to see you."

> *"Thanks for your part in ..."* (be specific: something they have done that contributes to the recent success of the enterprise.)

Listen to their response. Then ask:

> *"What are you working on today?*

"Sounds like you'll have a good day."

↰

Positive Attention Opens Doors

Kathy, department manager for an international telecommunications company, complimented her way to success:

"When I chose my 'Person Pearl' three weeks ago, I chose one of my own staff. I'll call her 'Jane.' 'Jane' was not performing at her full potential. She was also someone I really wanted to know a little better.

"When Jane first started in our department, she had been much more productive. I knew something had changed. I honestly didn't know how I was going to approach the subject with her. I'm still very uncomfortable dealing with such situations, especially if they have the potential to turn into confrontations. My primary concern was that she was not moving forward and improving. In fact, she was moving backward. Others who had started with our company at the same time as my 'Person Pearl' had moved up, and I knew she had the potential for expanded responsibility and advancement.

"I decided to pay more positive attention to what my 'Person Pearl' was doing. I went out of my way to compliment Jane when I overheard her handle a phone call especially well. I began to make it a point to compliment her when I noticed a problem was resolved in a quick and efficient manner. We are always under pressure with hard-to-meet deadlines. I was sure to comment when I thought my 'Person Pearl' had dressed especially nicely. I didn't overdo the attention, and I made sure the deed was always worthy of acknowledgment. I kept up the practice of offering positive comments for more than two weeks.

"Then one day, Jane asked to talk to me confidentially. During our private talk, she revealed a very serious problem that was taking place at her home. I listened quietly and attentively, and said I understood. We discussed how important it is that she should have my support. Then we went on to discuss how essential it was to separate our work from our private lives. I explained how Jane's attitude was affecting potential opportunities that could open up for her. Jane agreed that while at work, she would concentrate on her job. We discussed some of the options available to help resolve the home crisis. After that meeting, my 'Person Pearl' was greatly relieved, and instead of doing nothing about the home problem, as had been the case for the past two months, she made a decision to change her situation and followed through on it. I saw an immediate surge of energy.

↳ *"The lesson I learned from this experience is that paying attention and letting an associate know I am aware of their progress can open doors to improved performance."*

⇄

SECOND BASE: VOICING APPROVAL

Empowering leaders notice and acknowledge a job well done, and are quick to voice their approval. Too often, leaders comment only when something is overlooked, neglected or poorly executed. What must associates do to warrant approval? Conform, cooperate and comply, in accordance with agreed-to standards.

- ↻ "Thank you for completing this project on time;"
- ↻ "Thank you for wearing your safety glasses. You set a good example for others;"
- ↻ "It's great to see you following departmental guidelines, putting the labels on squarely;"
- ↻ "Keep up the good work!"

The following story is a wonderful example of how a working relationship, as well as a personal one, was improved through making an extra effort to provide approval.

⇄

Approval Wins Cooperation

Marlene, office manager for an industrial construction company, tried everything she could think of:

"I have had an ongoing problem getting purchase orders back to the office in a timely manner from project managers and field supervisors. Without the paperwork, I can't justify payments to our suppliers. This results in late payments, doubles the number of phone calls, lost paperwork and discounts. It wastes time, and, if taken to the extreme, could ultimately cost us our stellar credit rating, one of our important assets.

There is a lot at risk.

"The most troublesome to me was John. He never seemed to be able to get paperwork to me on time. I tried various methods—everything I could think of. I wrote notes. I paged him. I threatened to do awful things like not pay him. (Then, of course, didn't follow through on my threats.) One day, John left his cigarettes on my desk. I held them hostage and broke one cigarette for each day he made me wait for his purchase order paperwork. I still didn't get the paperwork from him on time. This, of course, caused us to clash even more.

"Then I decided to try the Turbo approach: *'Provide approval for what is working, and encouragement for the slightest improvement*.' I had nothing to lose except a little ego. I had always heard, 'You can catch more flies with honey than with vinegar.' So, one day, when he finally handed a purchase order to me on time, I commented on how much I appreciated his help and cooperation and the thoroughness of his notes of explanation. I kept it up, sending little comments of approval every time he was on time. Before long, to my amazement, he started getting all of his paperwork on time—even before the bills from suppliers came in! Wow! After only a few weeks, I rarely had to remind him.

↳*"The lesson I learned from this experience is that approval works. I learned that I can effectively get the behavior I want and the cooperation I need with positive, supportive feedback; and I learned that negative words, which are seen as criticism, only create* conflict."

NINETY-NINE APPROVAL PHRASES

1. You're on the right track now!	26. Totally awesome!
2. You've got it made	27. That's the best ever
3. Super	28. You've just about mastered it
4. That's right!	29. *PERFECT!*
5. That's good	30. That's better than ever
6. You're really working hard	31. You did that very well
7. You're very conscientious	32. Wonderful!
8. That's coming along nicely	33. You're making it happen!
9. GOOD WORK!	34. FINE
10. Great!	35. Nice going
11. I'm happy you're working	36. You're really going to succeed
12. Exactly right	37. Outstanding!
13. I'm proud of the way you work	38. FANTASTIC!
14. You're doing that much better	39. TREMENDOUS!
15. You've just about got it	40. That's how to handle it
16. That's the best you've ever done	41. Now you have the hang of it
17. You're doing a good job!	42. Marvelous!
18. THAT'S IT!	43. Way to go
19. Now you've got it figured out	44. You're doing fine
20. That's quite an improvement	45. Good thinking
21. That's coming along very well	46. You're really learning a lot
22. I knew you could do it	47. Good going
23. Congratulations!	48. Now you have it!
24. I like your attitude	49. You got_____right
25. Keep working on it	50. Good for you

51. Couldn't have done it better myself	76. Go for it!
52. Aren't you proud of yourself?	77. I'm very proud of you
53. One more time & you'll have it	78. Doesn't that look great!
54. You really make my job fun	79. I think you've got it now
55. That's the best way to do it	80. You can be very proud of this
56. You're getting better every time	81. Good job
57. You did it that time!	82. I like that
58. Couldn't have done it without you.	83. I've never seen anyone do it better
59. Go for the top	84. Keep on trying!
60. You haven't missed a thing	85. You outdid yourself today
61. WOW!	86. You figured that out
62. That's the way	87. You remembered!
63. Keep up the good work	88. That's really nice
64. Nothing can stop you now	89. You're improving
65. TERRIFIC!	90. You're the best
66. Atta girl!!	91. A-one effort
67. SENSATIONAL!	92. Go for it. You can do it
68. You've got your brain in gear	93. You did a wonderful job
69. I value your contribution	94. You'll go straight to the top
70. That was first-class work	95. You are really good at that
71. That kind of work makes me happy	96. You're the right one for this job
72. Keep it up!	97. You have a natural gift for this
73. You are learning fast	98. Positively superlative!
74. Your work habits are great	99. You are Number One
75. Well, look at you go!	

3. THIRD BASE: SHOWING APPRECIATION

When you make an investment, you hope it will appreciate in value. The truth is that when you *show appreciation*, your team members appreciate in value.

As an empowering leader, you are alert and aware of any extra effort people put into their work, providing superior service, coming in extra early or staying late. It is important that associates are aware of management's appreciation for what is going right. Show your appreciation by giving personal and public acknowledgment. It is a pretty good bet that if you don't give appreciation for extra effort when associates go beyond the call of duty, you will see them fall back in the ranks and just perform to minimum standards.

When someone submits an idea that helps the organization get over a major hump, say, "You're our hero! Thank you!" Your associates see themselves in the light of their strengths, making a valued contribution to something worthwhile, and strive to do even better.

Public acknowledgment encourages other associates to extend the extra effort needed to satisfy customers, cut costs, and improve quality. It is this additional contribution that helps create a winning championship team, one where each team member is committed to excellence and continually strives to improve their performance scores; where team members recognize each other's efforts, and have a sense of their own importance to the success of your organization.

APPRECIATION TIPS

Point out:

- ↻ How the team member recently showed extra-mile performance
- ↻ How they recently solved a perplexing problem
- ↻ How they provided additional value
- ↻ How their achievement contributes to the overall mission of the organization

> ⋛ **Whatever you reinforce, you will get more of.** ⋚

- ↻ "Thank you. I really appreciate your extra effort. Keep it up, and we will all win."

Don't Wait for a Convenient Time

Tom, design engineer for a lift truck attachment manufacturer, noticed great improvements:

"Early last Thursday, I took the opportunity to sit down and visit with my 'Person Pearl,' a member of my engineering team whom I'll call Maria. I had been looking forward to visiting with her because I had noticed some great improvements over the past month in her work habits and general attitude. I was eager to utilize Leadership Principle #4 -*Provide Empowering Acknowledgment.* I wanted to let Maria know that I had noticed her growth and improvement. I called her and set up a time for us to meet. Just before our morning meeting, I started getting butterflies in my stomach—I was really excited and a little nervous too!

"Our visit went very well, although we were both initially a little apprehensive. I believe my 'Person Pearl' thought she had done something wrong when I asked to visit with her in the conference room. I think she had expected a reprimand rather than acknowledgment. This made the initial atmosphere of the meeting a bit strange. I was a little uneasy because I was not sure how smoothly I was going to be able to communicate to her the sincere appreciation she deserved.

"After we began talking, it was interesting to see a very positive change occur in Maria's facial

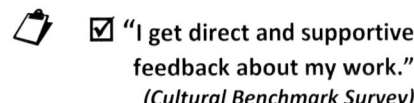

☑ "I get direct and supportive feedback about my work."
(Cultural Benchmark Survey)

expression and overall demeanor. It was apparent that she was at first surprised that I had taken the time to express my appreciation for the positive changes I knew she had been working hard to create. The atmosphere became a lot more relaxed as I, too, became less anxious about our meeting, and realized how truly easy it can be to offer sincere acknowledgment. I could tell my 'Person Pearl' appreciated the things I was saying. I was really making her day. I discovered that making her feel good made me feel good!

↳ *"The lesson I learned from this discussion is when I show my appreciation to a fellow team member, we both feel uplifted by the experience."*

4. HOME PLATE: PROVIDING PRAISE

You haven't made a home run until you cross home plate. You secure your home run by ***providing praise,*** which requires insight, and a courageous stretch. This is when you look deeper and zoom in on the desirable qualities you'd like to see more of beneath the surface performance. Effective praise is one of the best ways to nurture and encourage the growth of team members. Make sure your acknowledgment is immediate and specific. For example, you may say, "You have a strong sense of responsibility. I like the way you cleaned and organized your work station."

The empowering leader builds into the company's formal and informal conversations recognition and praise for a job well done. Remember, your most important job is to build people and make them successful. Praise helps your associates become more aware of their strengths, and gives them a reputation to live up to.

⇆

Praise Lights His Fire

Patrick, assistant manager of an automotive repair shop, "praised" the skinny kid into top performance:

"We hired a young man about a year ago. Jaman is a kind of tall, skinny, bashful kid. It was my job to train him in the way we do things, including the way we inspect cars, and how to write up estimates. He kind of just shuffled along in what he was doing. I let him work at his pace for a while to fully observe how he did things. I noticed how much knowledge Jaman had in areas that some of the rest of us were a little shy in. I realized he was fresh out of college, and really into certain aspects, like all of us were when we first got out of college. He just didn't seem to have any 'fire.'

"One day he came shuffling into work and I asked him if he had a moment, I wanted to talk to him for a minute. We weren't very busy that day, so I took him off to the side and said, `Jaman, I really admire the knowledge you have and the way you share it with us, the way you can, just by looking at the front or rear end of a truck as you walk by, tell all its specs, including its gear ratio. This knowledge can make you as valuable to us as any senior technician.' He smiled and turned a little red and said, 'Thank you.' I think I had unintentionally embarrassed him a little bit.

"At the end of the day, I told him he'd done a really good job and I'd see him in the morning. Well, the next day he came in and was moving faster and working quicker. He seemed more confident and friendly, and I thought, 'What's going on? This is a good thing.' He had a really good production day and he's been doing well ever since. It was great to see how a few words about how valuable and important he was to the shop because of his knowledge had lit him up.

↪*"I learned from this experience that expressing praise freely, with genuine interest, can help a new employee be as valuable as someone who has been with me for years."*

⇄

How to Give Empowering Praise

Empowering praise changes the way the receivers view themselves. Watch your associates. When you see someone demonstrate a praiseworthy trait, put the trait into a word, and tell your associate what you see, following the six-step praise process:

    ↻ Name the person receiving praise: "***Tom,***"

- ↻ Specify the quality or trait being praised: "you are— **persistent**."(creative, insightful, organized, original, courageous, supportive)

- ↻ Specify what they did that demonstrated the quality: "***You kept going! Most people would have quit.***"

- ↻ Describe how it contributed to success: "Your persistence helped us win the new customer, and in spite of the computer crash, we met our deadline."

- ↻ "As you continue to apply (quality cited above— persistence, creative, insightful, organized) in situations (specify future situation) like your new computer install project, you will succeed, and bring it in on time, too."

Then: . . . BE SILENT.

You will find daily opportunities to help your team see themselves as more capable, which is a giant step toward their growth, job satisfaction and greater contributions to your enterprise. Don't miss your opportunities to praise!

> ⋛ *Praise is empowering when it awakens the receiver to an awareness of their strengths.* ⋚
> –Unknown

The Unexpected: A Hand-Written Note

Jim, director of Produce for a food distribution company, transformed a low performer:

"Jon is a District Sales Rep for us in the Bend, Oregon area. He is one of our top sales associates but has continually had produce margins lower than most and several percentage points below our average. These low margins have gone on for over four years. I've taken extraordinary steps to arrange special workshops, group seminars, field training, all with him in mind. To be sure everyone really understood the facts, we worked with his District Sales Manager.

"We began to develop and furnish tracking numbers that showed which business sector our sales were coming from. The data showed trends to help Jon identify the best sales opportunities. We provided leads, tips, ideas and many specific examples of where others were getting added produce business with good margins. Nothing worked. His manager would just say, 'Well, you know Jon, he has a mind of his own.'

"After months and months of frustration, seeing the profit loss continue, I thought, 'What can I do differently?' (Thanks Turbo!) I decided to find at least one occasion where Jon had improved his margin on produce. It took a while. A couple of weeks later, as I was going through his numbers, I found that his margin was up .03 (hundredths) of a percent over his long standing average!

"I took out a piece of personal stationery and sent him a handwritten note of congratulation. Two weeks later, he was up .42 (hundredths) percent. I sent him another note. The next increase was over 2 percent! In the next note of congratulation, I added, 'Jon, you have proven to me that you are as good at merchandising for produce margins as you are at sales, and you're one of the best salesmen I have ever known.'

"A day later, he called me and said that he would treasure my note for the rest of his life and would keep it with his fondest mementos. Jon is not all the way yet, but he will get there.

↳ *"The lesson I learned from this experience is what a huge impact a few words of acknowledgment can make in the life of another person."*

⇆

Acknowledgment Is a Two-Way Street

Do you like receiving acknowledgment from 'the boss?' If you do, look around. You may realize that your boss never seems to receive praise. Make it a point to take time yourself to honestly and sincerely express appreciation to your supervisor. What you'll find is that when you make the effort to push recognition uphill, there will be a lot more up there to come back down!

Ken, comptroller for a general contractor, reverses the flow of recognition:

"Everybody wants to be praised, to have their achievements recognized and their positive attributes noticed. The company where I spent almost the last 10 years was very good at recognizing people and providing praise. After some time (OK, about 7 or 8 years – I'm a slow learner), I began to notice that even in a praise-enlightened organization, the flow seemed to be one way. The praise nearly always flowed downhill from supervisor to subordinate. I decided to see if I could expand the praise paradigm and reverse the flow.

"As Vice President, I reported directly to, and worked very closely with, the owners of the company. It wasn't hard to come up with a pretty good list of things to praise them for. They ran a great company with a truly unique corporate culture. They themselves were excellent praise-givers; they took excellent care of me and the other employees, and I truly appreciated them as people.

"So one day, I asked them to come into the conference room, closed the door, sat down across the table from them and announced that I had some remarks I wanted to make to them. I had prepared a nicely printed letter for each of them in which I explained how I felt about their many positive qualities and achievements I found praiseworthy.

"Needless to say, they were very surprised! It was really fun to watch them fidget nervously as I read each of the letters aloud. They deserved the praise, but because praise doesn't usually flow uphill, they were unaccustomed to receiving it. It turned out to be one of the most enjoyable meetings I can remember. Because we already had a good relationship, and because I was specific enough in my praise to preclude the appearance of flattery or 'brown-nosing', it worked out extremely well.

↳ *"What I learned from this experience is that while everyone needs recognition, the only way to make it happen for those 'at the top' is for it to come from down below. Since that day, I have made a practice of honestly appreciating my supervisor's personal qualities and achievements."*

⇆

What a marvelous example! You may have thought, "I can't imagine myself calling my bosses into a room with a letter and reading that letter to them, outlining the things I like, admire, and respect about them." Yes, it may be hard to imagine. For many of us, it would require more courage than we can muster. Ken is more courageous than most, and as he noted, he already had a great relationship with his managers. Your challenge is to exercise the courage it will take for you to praise your boss.

↩

HONE YOUR SKILLS

If you play golf, you know it can be a costly pursuit, involving equipment upgrades, professional advice and endless conversations with friends. As golfers analyze their game, watch other players and read golfing publications, their skills improve.

If managers took half as much interest in honing their acknowledgment skills as a dedicated golfer takes in improving their game, the results would be remarkable, says Fred Pryor. Those results may not always be tangible in the way improved golf scores are tangible. Yet, the manager who practices the art of providing sincere acknowledgment and expressing true appreciation for work well done will observe countless "intangibles" that contribute to productivity, retention and a positive workplace environment.

↩

SUMMARY

Actions for Empowered Leaders:

- ↻ Show genuine interest every day
- ↻ Practice Shoe Leather Leadership
- ↻ Provide the encouragement only you can give
- ↻ Give associates positive expectations to live up to

The Benefit You Will Gain:

- ↺ Your positive attention will open doors
- ↺ You and your team will be energized
- ↺ You will awaken team members' dormant potential
- ↺ You will secure the discretionary effort of your team

Chapter Ten

CONSTRUCTIVE COACHING

WHAT IS THE ANSWER?

Is one of your associates performing just a bit under par? Do you have the feeling that your department could be more productive? Have you noticed a gradual downward slide in attentiveness and energy? These feelings hovering in the back of your mind lead to frustration.

What is the answer? Constructive coaching. Constructive coaching is an important form of an empowering leader's feedback and feedforward communication. When an associate is struggling, or just doing things the hard way, coaching is the useful feedback only you can give to help them be more successful. Coaching is given with the intention of teaching and helping when people are not fully able to deliver up to their potential. Coaching calls upon all your communication skills to help ensure continuous improvement.

The old paradigm stated that we coach when a person is failing. The new paradigm says everyone is entitled to

> *Coaching: training by instruction, direction or demonstration for continuous improvement*

constructive coaching. The more capable you are in communicating coaching, the more of the team's capabilities you are able to tap. Through the process, the whole team rises to new heights.

Empowering leaders understand that coaching every member of their direct team is part of their "vital few." They set aside the time required for one-on-one communication and coaching to make sure their team is continually improving. Leaders lose talent when they neglect coaching. Associates who feel under-utilized and ignored, just coasting along or searching for new jobs elsewhere, can be found in most companies.

People-Focused Leaders

Pete, general division manager of an animal nutrition business, was only 15 years old when he landed a job at a feed company. His boss, the company founder, frequently asked him, "What are your plans for the future?" That first boss, who helped him get his present job, remains a close friend and role model.

Like him, Pete asks associates scores of questions to "learn how to serve them," he says. Five years ago, he was assigned to turn around a West branch of his company. The first thing he did was figure out which associates would excel at which jobs.

"In some corporations, if someone doesn't exactly fit one job, he's pushed aside for someone else," he adds. "I look at people as half full, not half empty, and try to find out what's happening to them at work and in their personal lives to find learning gaps that I can help fill."

Several years ago, observing a young associate as he spoke to a customer, Pete urged him to "act more like a prizefighter."

"Luke," he said, "I don't mind if you maybe get knocked down a few times, but you've got to have the confidence that I'm never going to let you get knocked out."

Now, Luke is himself a manager and tells his associates the same thing. "We're putting in eight–to-twelve–hour days, but we have fun. Because of Pete, it's a very tight-knit team with an almost family feeling," he says.

⇥

"The Best Feedback"

Lisa, business director of a wellness team, related her experience:

"My company had recently launched a new product line. I knew it would take an energized team to carry out a successful campaign. While still cheering on the star performers, I began to strengthen my team by giving special attention to those associates who appeared to need help. When someone is struggling, it's a huge drain on everyone else who must pick up the slack, so it's in my company's interests, and mine, to help that person.

"I feel great when my coaching helps an associate advance.

I coached one team member, who tended to 'charge headlong' into things, in how to confer more with other colleagues, a skill he needed to master. He later told me, 'It's clear that you and the company really care about my success.'

"*As a leader, that's about the best feedback I can ever get.*"

> ☑ **"I receive coaching that helps my performance continually improve."**
> (Cultural Benchmark Survey)

INFORMAL COACHING

Informal coaching can transform an average associate into a dynamic member of your team. Use informal coaching on an ongoing basis.

- ↻ Show how, then ask questions. Observing and "showing how" minimizes fears of criticism. Fear blocks learning.
- ↻ Coach in the context of your personal desire for each team member to reach their potential.
- ↻ Praise, praise, praise and recognition for what they are doing well.
- ↻ As coach, put yourself in the associate's place. If redirection is needed, meet one-on-one to point out what went wrong and how to make it right. (See Chapter Ten, Direction through Correction.)

Avoid making your associates wrong:

- ↻ Notice what worked and did not work during attempted performance. People listen when you are complimentary, and feel it is possible you can assist them.

Effective coaches are careful to avoid:

- ↺ Laughing at attempted performance
- ↺ Pointing out obvious mistakes
- ↺ Using praise followed by the fatal "But…" (And remember, "However" is just another way to say "but."}
- ↺ Overkill with more than one suggestion at a time

⇄

THE FOUR "P'S"™ OF EMPOWERING COACHING:

Praise, Permission, Performance, Prediction

Repeat with more and more finely tuned precision, as your team members' performance improves:

PRAISE

Tell them what they are doing well—spell out the specific, discrete aspect of the performance: "You are doing great on …" (**Now** *be specific—fit, or speed, or cleanliness, or organization.)*

PERMISSION

Ask permission to provide input: "I see a way that may help." Or, "I have an idea that might make things a little easier, or faster, or safer. May I mention it?"

PERFORMANCE

Focus on behavior, not on attitude. Explain clearly how you recommend they do the task differently. Show as you tell: "I recommend …" (*This is usually the easy part.)*

PREDICTION

Predict successful performance and practical outcomes with affirming comments: "You are going to be one of our best …;" "Soon you'll be twice as … *(fast, safe, effective.)"*

Jump for Joy

Ranae, merchandising manager for a wholesale food distributor, did her "homework:"

"Our family is in the process of opening a restaurant in Boise. The cash register my husband bought needed to be reprogrammed with all-new menu items and prices. Our 17-year old daughter is a computer whiz, so he assigned her the job of programming the till. She had no problem with the first fifteen items, but quit after that because the programming then required a combination of keys that didn't seem to work. She wanted me to take over and finish the job for her.

"This, unfortunately, is the usual sequence of events when Chelsie is given a big job. Chelsie refuses to challenge herself, push through the resistance, and put forth the extra effort needed to bring jobs to closure and fully complete the task. This, I realized, was my opportunity to practice empowering coaching.

"First, Chelsie and I had a talk about comfort zones. I explained to her that your personal comfort zone has an invisible wall around it. In order to get the feeling of victory, achievement and success we all want, you have to keep pushing against that wall and stretching it outward. This is how you grow and enjoy new experiences. Besides, if you don't push out those walls, they will shrink on you, and force you to live in a little, ever-smaller, contracting world. No fun!

"Then, when I felt I had her attention, I turned the manual for the cash register over and showed her the '800' number on the back. I suggested that she give the help desk a call and see if they could help her out; explain how to do the programming.

"The next day when I arrived home from work, she was skipping around, singing, 'I did it, I did it, I did it!' She had done just what I suggested, and managed to finish her job successfully. All the items were now programmed into the register. She was thrilled with herself!

↳*"The lesson I learned from this experience is that I can make people happier, more productive and less reliant on me by using empowering coaching. In addition, I free myself from having to do routine tasks. I want to jump for joy!"*

⇥

New Tricks for a Salty Old Dog

Steve, manager of delivery systems for an equipment manufacturer, accepted the challenge:

"At a session of the Leadership LAB, I was given the assignment of picking a 'Person Pearl' (a person I wanted to improve my relationship with) among my co-workers. I picked a supervisor—a rather salty dog—from within my managerial group. This supervisor had a history, a reputation of being a poor team player with his peers.

"As soon as I made this supervisor my 'Person Pearl', contact seemed to occur with ever-increasing frequency with almost no personal effort on my part. I began to make a continuous effort to find positive things about him to praise. I have worked hard at dealing with the frequent, somewhat negative issues much more swiftly. I moved past my tendency to procrastinate on the confrontational issues. I have been very careful to use our newly learned 4 P's Coaching process whenever possible. I have always made sure to start with praise and end with my stated belief in his capacity to complete work and be an exceptional team member.

"After a time, this salty supervisor was involved in a disagreement with one of his peers. They were arguing over who would perform a particular job on an ongoing basis. Things were escalating, so I called both of them to my office to discuss the situation privately. I made my expectations of cooperation and teamwork clear. After some heated discussion, an agreement was finally reached. I assured them both that I had confidence in their carrying out their parts of the agreement.

"About 30 minutes after the meeting ended, my 'Person Pearl' came back to say he felt the need to apologize to the other supervisor for his behavior during the earlier stages of our meeting. If I hadn't been seated, I might have fallen over. My 'Person Pearl' had grown! The corners were a little less rough, smoothed and polished up in some important places. He had taken the first step towards true maturity—accepting responsibility and accountability for his actions and for the outcome of his actions.

↳*"The lesson I learned from this experience is that if I am patient and persistent in my modeling of ideal behavior, I can teach even a salty old dog new tricks."*

⇌

Pass It On

Phil, fabrication shop foreman for a large general contractor, didn't give up:

"About a week ago, an apprentice came to me, asking if I would switch one of the workers on his crew over to another team. He told me the guy's inadequacy at installing fasteners was holding everyone and everything up.

"Instead of being too quick to give up on the situation, I decided to use Turbo's 4 P's for Positive Coaching model. First I wanted to be sure I was in rapport and that I was *appealing to his noble motives* (Leadership Principle #15). I said, 'I really appreciate your commitment to productivity while striving for quality and outstanding craftsmanship from yourself and others. Being highly productive with a quality product is how you and I and the company can compete, create and succeed.' (**Praise**)

"After establishing rapport, I was ready to begin the 4 P's Coaching process. I said, 'I have a suggestion that may help you in the short term and the company for the long term. May I mention it?' (**Permission**) His response was a predictable 'Yes!'

"I explained the 3-Step on-the-job training we practiced in the Turbo program. (*Note: See Chapter 12))* I said, 'Show your associate what you expect and how to do it; tell them why the quality and speed you expect is important; be hands-on as you explain the methods you use that will help speed up production; let them see you do it as you explain your method; ask them to explain to you what they are doing and why as they perform the task.' (**Performance**)

"Then I said, 'Give this approach a try. I think you will find a positive outcome.' (**Prediction**) 'Fair enough,' he replied, ' I just I hope it will work. We'll see what happens.'

"Toward the end of the day he came back to me and said, 'Thank you, you were right. Your training approach really worked amazingly well. My guy has been doing a great job all afternoon!'

↳*"The lesson I learned from this experience is that people are much more receptive to coaching when I start by asking their permission. Positive ↳feedforward*/feedback ↰ *is ten times more powerful than negative criticism. Being a coach and teaching others how to coach is very beneficial, with an empowering impact on the entire team."*

When a team is committed in true partnership, team members are unwilling to say or listen to anything unfavorable about one another. There is an ongoing respect for the progress of the team and what is in the best interest of each individual.

⇹

Look for the "Coaching Moment"

Tim, sales manager for a plating and finishing manufacturer, saw a great opportunity for coaching:

"When I saw a *Job Traveler* Mike had planned, I noticed that his customer was requesting a #125 machine finish on some flat bar material. Mike had written in the Notes section of the *Traveler* a note to the shop saying he wasn't sure what a #125

> ☑ **Our company is making significant improvements in quality."**
> -Cultural Benchmark Survey

finish was. If the operator in the shop didn't know either, he suggested, someone needed to go to the local tool store and buy a gauge that would tell them.

"Mike's intentions were good. He was trying to put the job in the shop as quickly as possible, so our customer would get their order in a timely manner. Unfortunately, in this situation, he was, in fact, slowing the process down by not providing all needed information for the shop up front.

"I knew this was a great opportunity to help Mike realize that the planning department is supposed to support and assist the shop in every way possible. This was an opportunity to reinforce the fact that we need to go out of our way to make sure we give others all the information that is necessary for them to do their job, and speed up response times to better serve our external customers.

"When I talked with Mike, he agreed that by taking an additional step himself, he could affect the timeliness and profits of orders, and, at the same time, eliminate a lot of unneeded job frustrations for the shop.

"Together we called down to our polishing department and asked if they could polish metal parts with different grades of emery belts. This was the additional information we needed in order to determine in the future what sanding belt would produce the customer's desired finish.

↳*"The lesson I learned from this experience is that I don't have to wait for a team member to make a mistake, or do something majorly wrong, before I step in and help. I can provide constructive, empowering, one-on-one coaching that creates opportunities for us to all improve almost every day."*

Coaching the Coach to Curtail Criticism

Jeff, district sales manager for a major food distributor, lets his Turbo coaching kick in:

"August 1st was the first day of my 10-year-old son's football practice. This is Josh's third year of tackle football. As always, there was the mandatory pre-season parents' meeting. This year the Maple Valley Football League has a new president. He introduced himself, spoke for a few minutes, and then announced that he had invited a guest speaker. The speaker was from a sports company that trains coaches on how to coach and also gives motivational seminars to organizations. He also was a coach for a national all-star basketball team of 14 to 15-year-old girls. "He told us that if we wanted to be good parents, we shouldn't watch our kids' practice. On his teams, parents aren't allowed at practices. His company had surveyed 1,300 kids who play sports in California. The number one complaint of these kids, what they hated most about organized sports, was the ride home from practice with their parents! The kids have just spent two hours being told about everything they were doing wrong and then get in the car with their parents, who spend the next 45 minutes on the ride home telling them, once again, everything they had done wrong. "WOW! A snapshot of my face popped into my head. I pictured Josh last year on our rides home, leaning against his door, trying to stay as far away from me as possible while I told him everything he had done wrong and what he should be doing instead. I felt about one inch tall! Then and there I decided I wouldn't do that again. I made a promise to myself, and to Josh, that I would have at least five positive things to say about his play after each practice.

"Scroll forward. It's Wednesday, and I'm trying to be a good parent attending Josh's practice. I saw Josh do two things that are fundamentally wrong, that resulted in his failure to block his man, allowing the player to make more tackles. I also noticed that none of the coaches were correcting Josh, so he continued to have the same problem. These were the same two things I'd told him he was doing wrong on our rides home last year.

"At the end of the practice, I ran up to Josh and told him, 'Great practice! I saw you …' and told him five things that he did correctly. Again I said, 'Great practice.' Then I let my Turbo training kick in. I looked at him and said, 'Josh, I saw two things that you might want to start doing that will help you in your blocking. Would you mind if I show you what they are?' He looked at me, smiled, and said he didn't mind.

"The next day at practice, I saw Josh really concentrate on trying to do the two things I showed him, and he was doing much better at blocking his man.

"This year has been entirely different for Josh and me. I've been keeping my promise. When practice is finished, I immediately go over to Josh and tell him five things he did right. Now, after practice, he comes over to me with a smile on his face instead of a frown. Afterwards, he even asks for constructive feedback instead of flinching when I give it.

↳*"The lesson I learned from this experience is that positive influence creates positive action."*

One of the reasons we lack communication and understanding is our reluctance to talk about issues that bother us. We learned in childhood not to "rock the boat," not to bring up the unpleasant, the discomforting. Some of us have learned to discuss the disagreeable only when things get so bad that we lose our tempers. The fear of discussing difficult issues further isolates us from real communication, understanding, and relationships.

Any Time is the Right Time for Coaching

Doug, scaffold manager for a heavy equipment company, grabbed the moment:

"I was leaving our back lot, getting ready to head for home, when I noticed the inefficient process two of our yard men were going through as they counted a pallet of scaffold assembly parts to be returned to our inventory.

"There was a man on each end, counting items on the pallet. I couldn't help doubting the accuracy of this method. It looked to me like some items were going to be counted twice and maybe some were going to be missed entirely. I approached Todd on the dock and asked him if he had ever been told about the importance of 100 % accuracy in counting returned parts that

> *≥We only go around once. There's really no time to be afraid. Try something you've never tried. Teach it. Do it. Risk it.≥*
> --John Blais

will be reintroduced into inventory. He kind of shrugged and said, 'Yeah, sort of.' I asked him if I could offer three steps that would make the job a little easier and a lot more accurate. 'Sure,' he said.

"'One, sort the gear into piles of like equipment;' I suggested; 'Two, count the individual piles, and Three, Re-stack the piles onto pallets of like equipment.'

"I explained that this process accomplishes three objectives at the same time: 'First, it provides an opportunity to check each piece of equipment for quality so that we don't send out broken or unsafe scaffolding parts to the next job.

"'Secondly, we get accurate counts so we don't have frustrating shortages at job sites, or have to order more pans than we really need just in case. Shortages cost us labor time and can cause delays that keep us from meeting our agreed-to completion date on projects. This upsets our customers and all of the trades that depend on us to do our job first.

"'Third, the gear is put away properly. In other words, we can find what we need when we need it.'

"Todd said, 'Looks like it will take a lot more time, but I can see it will be worth it.' As I drove home, I felt a lot better than I would have if I had just walked on by, calling them names under my breath.

↳*"The lesson I learned from this experience is to observe the processes and methods of those around me, to take advantage of an optimum coaching moment when it arises and provide the training needed in a constructive way."*

Football Dilemma Provides Lesson for Business

Our oldest son Larry Jr. called this morning with very surprising news. Our 9-year old grandson, Tyler, didn't want to play football anymore. I was shocked to hear this because less than a week ago Larry told me that while he was driving Tyler to football practice Tyler was singing "I love football, I love football, I love, I love, I love football!" He has grown more and more excited about football as the season grew closer.

Larry went on to tell me the reason Tyler didn't want to play football anymore was because the coaches, the persons who are responsible to train, equip and motivate the first year players, were "hollering" at him. This is a 9-year old, who before they started yelling at him, was very motivated. Even though he is one of the shortest guys on the team, he is solid muscle and grit. Last year, his soccer team won every single game they played—22 wins, no losses. Tyler scored a lot of the winning points, and was the enthusiastic spark plug of the team.

Larry wanted to know what to do and how to respond. We both agreed that he can't make Tyler play football and we don't want to spoil Tyler's joyous spirit. Of course Larry needed to help Tyler not to take it personally, to simply understand that this behavior on the part of his coaches is simply because they are frustrated and don't know how to communicate in a way that is respectful to motivate and win. They may have the best intentions, but they don't understand how to motivate.

The Voice of Experience

My experience in training over 4,000 entrepreneurs, managers and supervisors has shown me that these kinds of unskilled tactics are still in play in the world of business. Unskilled managers, trying to motivate, "holler" at their team members. Their comments are interpreted as, "I'm under attack."

Many of us, when we become frustrated, resort to behaviors that are not skillful. These unskilled behaviors fail to get the desired results. The command-and-control style of management is brought back into play. Even though command and control may get compliance, it also can lead to resentment. The team member may not refuse to go back to work, like Tyler, but they do refuse to do anything extra. They refuse to bring you any new ideas, and cease to engage themselves creatively. They no longer volunteer those little extras which create superior customer service in an increasingly competitive world.

The best advice I can give you is to observe your own behavior; don't resort to yelling at team members. Observe the behavior of those on your team who are supervising to ensure that they are never seen as attacking fellow team members. Should that belittling behavior occur, I urge you to find a way to immediately get to the bottom of things, and eliminate demeaning behaviors that can result in lackluster performance.

Provide supervisory team members with the training they need to ensure that their leadership style is always empowering. The kind of leadership that truly is motivational and inspiring results in creativity, cooperation and commitment.

P.S. Tyler did go back to practice and at his next game, and not only did he play, he played exceptionally well, including two full body tackles that brought the opposing carrier down and won a decisive victory for Tyler's Cardinals. Yea!

SUMMARY

Actions for Empowering Leaders:

- ↻ Stop, look and listen for opportunities to coach
- ↻ Start by making a specific, positive observation
- ↻ Ask permission to make constructive suggestions
- ↻ Limit your suggestion to one idea
- ↻ Always end on a positive note

The benefits you will gain:

- ↻ Your associates will look forward to seeing you
- ↻ Your team will emulate your behavior
- ↻ Your best people will continue to improve
- ↻ You will develop improvement consciousness
- ↻ You will have a high-performance team

Chapter Eleven

DIRECTION BY CORRECTION

CREDIBLE CONSISTENCY

One of the most common complaints is the feeling that discipline is not consistently applied to all. To be consistent, two things must occur:

All associates must be clear about the standards; all managers must be consistent in communicating and enforcing the standards equitably.

Why aren't managers consistent in the discipline of poor performers? Fear of confrontation. Giving in to the fear of confrontation results in substandard performance and loss of the respect of your team. Providing consistent correction and discipline helps you create a culture of accountability. Moving past excuses and a tolerance for lackluster performance, you turn non-performance into a deep learning experience that ensures immediate and lasting improvements.

↤
↦

Consistent Corrective Feedback Creates Consistent Performance

Tom, team leader in a machine shop, holds the line for performance standards:

"Two weeks ago, I looked up from my work and noticed my Level Five machine operator over at another person's machine, talking to the other operator. I was losing the production time of two of my key operators. As I approached Jimmy, I got a feeling in my gut that I really didn't want to do what I was about to do. I reminded myself of what I'd learned in the Leadership LAB, and the feelings started to subside.

"'Jimmy,' I said, 'could you do me a favor?' He said, 'Yes, if I can.'

"I went on, 'I've noticed you over the past couple of days spending a lot of time visiting with other operators at their machines.' He jumped right in my face, yelling, 'I get out 100% of target with no errors; I should have the right to do as I please.'

"I replied, 'Jimmy, that's great! I appreciate the high quality of your work and your commitment to meeting our department's production standards.' I went on, 'Since you are one of my Level Five team members, I need you to set a positive example for the rest of the crew.'

"His face returned to its normal color and he moved back out of my face. I said to him, 'I really do count on you.' He replied, 'Yes, I can do what you ask.' Then I left.

"A few minutes later, Jimmy came over to my area and told me he was sorry for getting in my face. He explained that he was mad at himself for letting this problem go long enough that I was forced to talk to him about it.

↳ *"The lesson I learned from this experience is that when it comes to holding my team accountable to agreed-upon performance standards, I need to 'just do it.' I learned that when I confront the fears that fly around inside of me, they go away. I learned that when I take charge of my own attitude, I can shape the attitudes of my team."*

⇤⇥

STAND UP FOR STANDARDS

You won't believe this story! An engineer was being disciplined for crashing his

> *There is no excuse for unacceptable behavior.*
> —Jack Boland

locomotive through a receiving door of the warehouse. He responded by saying, "There is nothing in the policy manual that says you're not supposed to drive the locomotive through that door."

There is a right way and a wrong way to do most everything. There are policies and procedures that spell out some of these standards; others are a "given." It is a given that we treat one another respectfully; behave as adults; keep our agreements; clean up our mess; keep others informed when we can't deliver as agreed; and when we break something, report it quickly. The list goes on. The point is that there are protocols and standards that we must adhere to to function as a high performance team that may not be documented in a policy manual.

"There is no excuse for unacceptable behavior." As a supervisor at any level, from CEO to frontline foreman, you have a serious responsibility to respond to all unacceptable behaviors—acceptably. It follows that when you observe unacceptable behavior, there is no excuse for you to resort to unacceptable behavior in dealing with it.

Let's look at two unacceptable ways of responding to unacceptable behavior. The first is to ignore the behavior and hope it will get better—pretend you didn't see it; "it isn't that important;" "she didn't know any better;" "he's having a bad day." This avoidance of your responsibility shows weak leadership, and leads to confusion and low morale.

The second is reacting in anger, losing your temper, dramatic displays of upset. These are signs of immaturity and lack of self-control, and just as unacceptable as the behavior you are trying to correct. Yes, there may be times to raise your voice and speak sternly. There is never a time to lose your temper. If and when you do, you lower yourself to the level of the one you are correcting. You lose the respect of the team.

We've all said, "That makes me so mad!" "Mad"—a word defined by Webster as *to craze; to excite with violent passion; to enrage; furious; wild.* When you're mad, you've lost touch with reason. You know what they do with mad dogs—they shoot them; and you know where they put "mad" people—they lock them away. Anytime you and I are "mad," it might be appropriate to lock *us* up!

The point here is not that we should not express negative emotions; expressing upset may be necessary for us to live normal, balanced lives. As mature adults, we need to let trivial things, the "toothpaste-squeezed-at-the-wrong-end," go. Response to unacceptable behavior must be expressed quickly, appropriately, professionally, in an acceptable, timely fashion, not stuffed. Stuffing your negative feelings can ultimately result in explosive behavior.

Tempered steel is hard; tempered steel keeps its edge. It has great strength; it's strong, sharp and valuable. Overheated steel loses its temper; it loses its strength; it can no longer keep an edge. This is what happens to us when we get overheated. We lose our "edge" when we lose our temper; we lose our competitive edge, we lose the edge of a winning team committed to results.

⇄

DEALING WITH UNMET STANDARDS

Discuss unfulfilled expectations openly and honestly. Tell your associates your goal is to help them do the best job possible and perform to

> *He has the right to criticize, who has the heart to help.*
> --Abraham Lincoln

their highest capability. When a performance situation arises, discuss the situation immediately.

When a tune-up or adjustment is called for:

If the associate **did not know how to perform**:
use the **Four-P's of Coaching™** (See Chapter 10, *Coaching,* or the **Six T's™ of Training,** Chapter 12, *Seeing How To.*)

If the associate **did know how to perform**, **and chose not to:**
use the **DARE ✚ Correction Process™** which follows.

When you apply this six-step formula for holding team members accountable for failing to perform to agreed-to-standards, you turn the failure into the constructive, cognitive learning lesson required to ensure future agreements are kept and standards are met.

The *DARE* ✚ Correction Process™

▶ *DARE*

Describe the observed unacceptable behavior

Ask what happened and listen carefully to the response

Restate the agreed-to standard

Emphasize the reason the standard is important

▶ *PLUS*

✚ Ask for their agreement to comply with the standard

✚ End on a positive note

Now let's look at several examples of how to apply this formula to correct associates who have violated agreed-to performance standards:

Late to Work—Again

Ron, store manager for a regional sporting goods retail store, finds a timely solution:

"Just this morning at 9:30 AM, as I was standing at the front of the store, I noticed that one of my star cashiers was not at her check stand. She was scheduled at 9:30 and I knew that she already had a record of attendance problems. She walked in 15 minutes later.

"As soon as we could cover the register with another checker, I asked her to come upstairs to my office with me where we could discuss her attendance privately.

"When we got to the office:

(▶ DARE)

Describe. "I told her I noticed she came in 15 minutes

late, and pointed out that she already had a record of repeatedly being late.

Ask. "I then asked her, 'What happened?'

Restate. "I reminded her of our company commitment to punctuality. She really seemed to care about getting here on time and appeared to feel bad about being late.

Emphasize. "I reminded her of why punctuality is essential to teamwork and maintaining superior customer service, both of which are values we are committed to. I told her that I valued her as an associate and wanted to make sure she understood the importance of being at work on time."

(▶ PLUS)

+ "I said, 'You're an excellent associate, great with the customers, and I know you can get here on time.' She committed to making the arrangements needed to be on time in the future. I said, 'I have faith in you and am sure you will be able to be here on time and avoid further problems with attendance.'"

⇤

Options for Action

When you observe people whose performance falls below standards, you have three options.

Option 1, ignore the behavior, talk about the behavior behind their backs or to yourself, and hope it'll get better. This approach makes you a victim, and if the performance improves, it is a matter of luck, not leadership.

Option 2, attack, diminish, belittle or demean the associate who has committed the infraction. When you attack, your ego may feel better momentarily. This attempt to prove who's boss usually creates less value in the long term than saying nothing, and can result in reduced teamwork and even sabotaging behaviors.

Option 3, the highest possible action you can take, the ***DARE ✛* Six-Step Corrective Process**, the action Ron models so well in the story above.

⇄

This Stuff Really Works!

Ray, service manager for an auto repair company, demonstrates:

"I have a team member who was not covering his one night a week on-call shift. I brought him into my office, asked him to sit down, and began to use the ***DARE✛*** **Correction Process**:

(▶ *DARE)*

Describe observed behavior. "Ricardo, I see that you have been missing your on-call shifts."

Ask what happened. "I listened attentively as Ricardo explained that he had missed the first time because it was his wedding anniversary. He and his wife had been out celebrating, which included a little more drinking than he had planned, and he knew it would be a violation of policy to drive a company vehicle under the influence of alcohol. The second time he missed, it was because his brother was ill and needed his help. "

Restate the agreed-upon standard. "I reminded him that each assigned associate is to cover their weekly on-call shift."

Emphasize the reason for the standard. "If you don't make your scheduled shift, it creates a hardship for other team members. If you need a schedule change for special occasions, we can always make the needed arrangements with advance notice." I then told him to call a team member at the shop and let them know as soon as he knew there would be a problem covering his shift.

(▶ PLUS)

✛ "I asked Ricardo if he was willing to agree to our standards, follow the procedure of calling in or changing his shift if he had a conflict in the future; otherwise, to make all of his scheduled on-call shifts. Ricardo promised that he would follow procedure and keep his shift in the future. If an emergency did arise, he would let another team member know at the earliest possible opportunity.

✛ "I told him with emphasis and a smile that he is an important part of our team.

↳ *"The lesson I learned from this experience is that the* **DARE ✛ Correction Process** *really works. It gives me a track to follow so I don't get engaged in attacking, justifying or arguing."*

The Job Isn't Done till the Paperwork Is In

Paul, operations manager for a scaffolding erection company, changes his methods and helps an associate:

"Paperwork accuracy is crucial to the efficiency and success of our operations. I have made many mistakes over the years learning this area of our business. Willie, one of our carpenter foremen, is a

> ⸙*Correction communicates the intention of directing associates in performing up to their capabilities.*⸙

fantastic worker, always willing to go the extra mile to complete a project. Unfortunately, the quality of the paperwork he was submitting at the end of the day was substandard. We have had previous conversations as well as training sessions, going over every detail of the paperwork, but nothing seemed to last very long. 'There isn't enough time,' as well as other excuses, was his justification for the incomplete paperwork. I resigned myself to the fact that he was not going to be able to qualify for the foreman position if I had to continually correct and complete his paperwork.

"I was already involved in the Leadership Lab, learning many new ways to talk with, help, and instruct my team. I knew I would have to change my methods in order to help Willie make the necessary improvements. Soon an opportunity arose for me to apply my new-found learning.

"Willie had submitted incomplete paperwork again! This time, I used the *DARE* ✚ Correction Process:

(▶ *DARE)*

Describe unacceptable performance: "Willie, I see you submitted incomplete paperwork yesterday.

Ask what happened: "I listened intently to the response as he began some of the excuses I had heard in the past.

Restate the standard: "'As you know, it is the foreman's responsibility to have the paperwork completed accurately by the days' end.'

Emphasize the reason for the standard: "'The important reason for the standard is that the data entry into the computer must be done on a daily basis. The accuracy and timeliness of both determine inventory availability and customer billing accuracy.'

(▸ *PLUS)*

> ✦ **Commitment to agreement:** "'By taking extra time at the end of the day, will you be able to complete your paperwork on time and maintain your foreman position?' Willie agreed to comply with the standards.

> ✦ **End on a positive note:** "'Willie, you are one of our very best. You always go the extra mile on the job. I'm sure you will be able to complete the paperwork accurately the next time out!'

"It took just a few seconds to state in understandable terms what I had been trying to say to Willie for months.

↳ *"The lesson I learned from this experience is that effective correction begins with me and is a continuous process within myself as well as with others."*

↹

DEALING WITH DIFFICULT BEHAVIOR

Consider this approach when you interact with associates whose behavior is difficult to deal with:

"Kill" with kindness. Treat others well, regardless of how they treat you. Be direct, polite and professional. It's hard to treat a thoughtful person thoughtlessly.

Listen and respond. Allow the difficult person to fully express all their feelings.

Acknowledge your awareness of the situation, describe what you see and hear, reveal what you think and feel. Tip: Don't judge ("You shouldn't be that way") or generalize ("You always do that.")

Don't take a position; rather, deal with their need. Find out what motivates them so you can offer alternative ways of solving the problem. Chances are the difficult person confronting you has simply adopted the most obvious solution. In other words, move from what the person wants to why the person wants it.

Accept blame. More often than not, you have played some role in bringing about the undesirable behaviors. Admit your fault quickly and empathetically. When you shoulder your share of the blame, others are more likely to own up to theirs. Tip: Sometimes, by claiming more responsibility than you deserve, you can encourage the other person to cooperate.

Who, Me?

> ⸮Let me never fall into the vulgar mistake of dreaming that I am persecuted whenever I am contradicted. ⸮
> —Ralph Waldo Emerson

There are going to be days, and we have all had them, when a coworker, friend or family member lashes out at you for no predictable reason. Coworkers and clients obviously have the liberty to behave badly toward you at will. It is important to realize the likely consequences of your reactions, whether inadvertent or deliberate. Silent victims of out-of-control people often suffer both acute and chronic effects from demeaning treatment. You have freedom in your choice of reactions.

Let's remember Isaac Newton's Third Law of Motion: "For every action, there is an equal and opposite reaction." Is a coworker's blatant hostility resulting in pent-up hostility in you? Could your hidden anger be silently "screaming" back at the associate through angry eyes, set mouth and jaw, tone of voice and resentful body language?

You are the catalyst in lessening the hostility in your relationships. When your reaction is neither overtly nor covertly hostile, it leaves others in the position of a tennis player playing tennis alone—there is no incentive to keep serving a ball that is not being returned.

When the angry associate calms down, discuss the situation. Make it clear that you will not accept behavior that violates your personal dignity. You can always start with, "You're having a really bad day, aren't you? Do you want to tell me more about it?"

↹

Workplace Whining

Few things are more annoying than whining co-workers. They constantly point out problems but never act to improve the situation. To make matters worse, their negative comments and muttering can have a serious effect on the morale and productivity of those around them. To minimize whining:

- ↻ Listen carefully. Give whiners a few minutes to vent. They may be simply trying to relieve tensions. As they unburden to a sympathetic ear, they frequently come to realize that the matter is really only a small annoyance. The result is often that whiners talk themselves right out of the gripe.
- ↻ Keep your composure. If you lose your temper or show hostility, the whiner may respond in kind. A

heated argument will only worsen the situation.

↻ Don't dismiss the whining too quickly. There's a strong possibility that a trivial complaint could be a cover-up for a real problem. If there's something you can do to resolve the complaint, do it. If the subject of the whining can't be fixed, ask whiners to come up with solutions to problems that can be corrected. Help them see that their complaints affect the morale and energy of the whole team, and in actuality, their comments are a bigger problem than the situation they are whining about.

Time Out for the Gossiper!

To condemn is to consider some-one guilty, to judge, to blame; to pronounce someone bad, wrong, or unacceptable.

Here's a way to stop the condemning gossip.

When any person comes to you condemning, gossiping about another team member, say, "Time out! I'm a little uncomfortable talking about this. Have you talked with (Sally) about it?"

If their answer is "no," which it often will be, add, "I recommend you talk to them directly." (Leadership Principle #3 - *Don't Criticize, Condemn, or Complain.*)

No Excuse for Blue Language

Gary, supervisor for an equipment manufacturer, handled profanity this way:

"One of the unit specialists in my area was overheard

saying to a machine operator, 'What the *!* X # ?* are you doing?' This language is not allowed at our company, nor is it tolerated. I decided the best way to handle the situation was to provide the unit specialist with some obviously needed correction and coaching. I issued a written warning for his behavior.

"I called the unit specialist into my office to discuss the incident. He was shocked when I

> *Speak when you're angry, and you'll make the best speech you'll ever regret.*
> —Lawrence J. Peter

handed him the written warning. As he read it, his face turned red. His uncalculated response was, 'I'm sorry.' I could tell he was sincere.

"We talked about the incident, and explored the events that led to his outburst of profanity. When I was sure he knew that I understood how provoking some of the operators can be, we did some role-playing of appropriate ways to correct an operator without resorting to profanity. I asked him to play the part of the operator, who had made a mistake, as I played his role. We practiced ways of responding constructively, professionally, and proactively to various situations that arise in our shop.

"Through this exercise, the unit specialist began to discover that the operator he had cursed was merely in need of coaching and correcting—not a harsh, vulgar scolding. He learned that when you swear at someone who has made a mistake you only instill in them fear, anger and confusion. By providing them with effective feedback, you are professionally confronting the problem, constructively solving it through instruction, and proactively preparing for future similar situations.

"The unit specialist agreed to apologize to the operator involved, and to all the operators on the floor for his use of offensive language. He followed through on his commitment to apologize that morning. Before the day was over, I could see that his reputation had already begun to improve."

⇆

Do It Right the First Time

Keith, credit manager for an auto rental service, decides not to let it slide:

"Our company uses a networked contact management system called 'Goldmine' to track sales activities, collection calls, and various customer service matters. The credit department relies on the accuracy and completeness of this information for making collection contacts. We count on Goldmine to have all the important information we need for each customer so we know who to call when an account is past due.

"In the past, I have not always held associates accountable when I've noticed the person responsible for accounts payable is not named in the database. Instead of reminding the associate of the standard of always entering a name for the accounts payable contact in the database, I would step in and either make a 'cold call,' asking for the in-charge person; research previous calls; or go to the credit card file to determine an appropriate contact name and telephone number. After taking the time and effort required to get this information, I would enter it into Goldmine myself. It didn't usually seem to take all that long.

"Last week, I was following up on a call from one of our collectors, and again there was no contact name in Goldmine. Rather than 'let it slide,' I decided to address the matter with my collector. I asked her what happened. Before I could even finish the process of corrective feedback, she was on the computer fixing the problem. She explained that sometimes she gets so busy with a telephone call that she forgets to go back and enter the contact name when the call is completed. She obviously knew the standard. I reminded her how much it helps associates making follow-up calls when she takes a short moment at the time of her contact to complete this simple step. My corrective feedback was non-confrontational and well received.

↳ *"The lesson I learned from this experience is that when I consistently hold associates accountable to agreed-to standards, it relieves me of the responsibility of finishing the associate's job, and saves me the time and waste of duplicated effort. Associates realize that I care about their performance and I am not on the receiving end of 'reverse delegation'."*

↹

Team Passes Inspection

James, produce director for a food distributer, holds associate accountable:

"Early in November, Beth, whose responsibilities included proper inspection of all incoming produce, failed to inspect a load of tomatoes. Unfortunately, they were accepted and received by our produce center anyway. It was determined the following day that the entire load had 40% to 50% decay, a potential loss of several thousand dollars. This was a very serious situation.

"To complicate matters, Beth had already given notice that she was leaving our firm in a month to pursue a new career. The easy thing for me would have been to forget it, and then grumble and complain, 'You just can't count on anyone anymore.' I ruled this out, in part because of the serious impact on costs and loss of profit. More importantly, this oversight on Beth's part had the potential for creating a serious problem in customer satisfaction. I knew this was the time to use the *DARE* ✝ Correction Process. So I met with Beth and began:

(▸ DARE)

Describe observed behavior. "You apparently missed inspecting the important tomato shipment."

Ask what happened. "I asked her what happened and waited for her response. She said that the warehouseman had put them away before she got there to inspect them.

Restate the standard. "'You are aware that our policy states that you must visually inspect all incoming produce, aren't you?' I waited for her acknowledgement that this is a policy she is aware of. She agreed.

Emphasize the importance of the standard. "I explained the important reason for our policy of inspecting all incoming produce so that we don't suffer financial loss or deliver bad product to our customer, causing them inconvenience and unnecessary expense. She gave her commitment to fulfill every part of her job responsibilities.

(▶ PLUS)

✚ "I affirmed to her that she had been an important part of our team and that even though she is leaving, we want her to stay focused and do a proper job so she can leave feeling good about herself and the job she has done for us. She said, 'You're right, I do want to leave with good feelings.'

↳ *"The lesson I learned from this experience is the importance of not giving in to temptation and avoiding my responsibility to hold everyone accountable to agreed-to standards."*

↤↦

Inappropriate Correction Calls for Correction

Here is an example of what can happen with an inappropriate correction of an associate:

Eileen, training, safety and recruiting manager, was surprised and let down:

"A few weeks ago, as we began our Friday morning staff meeting with all of our department managers, one of the managers asked if she could make the suggestion that the staff meeting also be a forum for problem-solving and making group decisions. She went on to say that the benefit would be that the team could

> ≳ *Praise in public, hold accountable in private.* ≲

decide on issues affecting everyone. At first, no one objected. Everyone seemed to think it sounded like a good idea. Then she went on to say, '... instead of situations like when Eileen didn't consult any of us and adjusted the background music so low no one can hear it.'

"I was taken by surprise, and let down, that she didn't approach me ahead of time to warn me that she was going to use me as a 'bad' example in front of the rest of the team. The room went silent. No one knew how to respond. Of course her suggestion was not followed, because the good idea was lost in its delivery. Everyone was focused on me, waiting for a reaction or response to this public slap on the wrist. It was awkward for us all.

↳ *"The lesson I learned from this experience is to never correct or use someone else as a bad example in public. Although it is acceptable and can be quite effective to publicly draw attention to my own mistakes, others should never be 'put down' in public."*

The creation and maintenance of a championship team that supports and cares for each other is no small task. The benefits gained from a sense of belonging always result in enhanced performance. The true leader who genuinely cares about the team and each member on it will think before speaking and exercise the courage required to confront in private, in a constructive way.

Remember this simple principle: Praise in public, hold accountable in private. By following this guideline, you lead from high ideals and gain respect.

Sometimes, a Job Just "Stinks"

Gary, machining supervisor for an equipment manufacturer, handled a smelly situation:

"About three months after I became a machining supervisor, a delicate situation began to develop concerning one of my machine operators. A few of my team members had commented to me about one particular operator's body odor. This was a problem that I had never had to face in the workplace, nor had I foreseen it arising in my new supervisory position. It was just one of those strange situations that no one thinks about needing to deal with.

"I wanted to check out the situation for myself, so I headed toward the operator's work station to speak to him. As I approached his general vicinity, I could smell the odor in question. It was bad enough to singe nose hairs! I knew I was going to have to address this problem quickly, with utmost delicacy.

"I took a few steps back out of the area, and thought about how to approach the problem. I spoke with a few other supervisors and got some ideas on how to handle the situation. I made a decision to speak to the operator the very next day.

"On the next day, I approached the operator, and told him that I needed to talk to him. He came into my office and sat down. I decided to be honest and let him know how I was feeling from the start of this conversation. I told him that I had something to talk to him about, and I was very uncomfortable discussing it with him. I then cut to the chase and said that a few of the operators and unit specialists have complained about his body odor.

"I went on to tell him about some of the problems this caused. I reminded the operator that he was in the process of learning a new machine, which required some close training with others in the shop. If his body odor prevented people from providing training, he would not learn as much or as fast as he could. I also asked if his body odor was a chronic problem, and mentioned that if so, he should see a doctor. I told him the benefit he would gain would be better training from unit specialists and operators.

↳ *"The lesson I learned from this experience is that even if the topic is an extremely uncomfortable one, I must address it and I have the ability to do so. When such a situation arises, it must be addressed, although no one enjoys this type of personal confrontation."*

↤
↳|

PROGRESSIVE DISCIPLINE

In a Union environment, you must have a form of progressive reprimand and discipline. One of the excuses or reasons for not providing correction or initiating progressive discipline is that supervisors feel they won't be backed up by management or the human resources department.

Though the *DARE ✛ Correction Process*™ presented in this chapter is not part of the reprimand process, the principle still applies. There's no excuse for unacceptable behavior. If unacceptable behavior persists after you have utilized the correction process, it will be necessary to initiate your company's formal progressive discipline process. As a general rule, the six steps of the *DARE* ✚ model would not be considered verbal. Your formal verbal will be documented, and would normally follow what we've presented here.

ᴴ↹ᴵ

SUMMARY

Actions for Empowering Leaders:

- ↻ Consistently hold your associates responsible
- ↻ Quickly face up to aggressive people
- ↻ Use the *DARE* + Correction Process
- ↻ Remember, any and all unacceptable behavior is unacceptable
- ↻ Always talk in private when correcting behavior

The Benefits You Will Gain:

- ↻ You will feel better about yourself
- ↻ You will earn the respect of your team
- ↻ Your team's moral will go up
- ↻ You will see improved performance

Chapter Twelve

SEEING "HOW TO"

"HOW-TO" COMMUNICATION

Many productive team members feel they are a valuable part of the organization; there are others who do not appear to be fully engaged. The difference lies in the quality of the leadership they receive. Leaders who focus on talent assign associates to jobs that play to their strengths, make sure they have the resources they need to perform well, respect their opinions and challenge them to advance.

In employee survey after survey, learning "how-to" is one of the most frequent requests we hear from associates and managers alike. These folks aren't asking for training in basket-weaving or rocket science; they just want to be shown how, to do what they are being paid to do.

Why aren't those training needs being met? I don't understand. How could you expect to maximize results without providing associates with the knowledge

> ☑ **"Our training equips us all to succeed."**
> — *(Cultural Benchmark Survey)*

and skills necessary for them to successfully perform their jobs?

Surprisingly, the same supervisors and managers who are failing to provide adequate training for their teams are often coaching youth sports teams in their off hours. They proudly tell us how they helped the kids sink a basket, slide for second, throw a block, shoot a puck. Why aren't these supervisors providing this same level of support in the fundamentals of job performance for their team members on the job?

Does it make sense to put people in a role they haven't been adequately trained and equipped for? How can we justify putting a person in a job where they can't succeed? Believe me, I've heard all the excuses: "We don't have enough time;" "There's so much turnover it doesn't make sense to train people because they will only leave us anyway;" (That's an interesting excuse, isn't it?) "If they can't figure out how to do it, maybe they don't fit here;" and, worst of all, "No one ever trained *me*."

If you're waiting for your talent director to provide the help your team needs to perform at a higher level, you are missing the point. You must find ways, as an engaging leader, to provide the meaningful one-on-one input your team needs now. You are the one who clarifies roles, describes what excellence looks like and how to get it done. You are the one that instructs in what they must do to be successful. This is ↳*feedforward*/feedback↰ in its highest form.

OFF YOUR SEAT, ON YOUR FEET

> ⸮ *To hear is to forget; to see is to remember; but to do is to understand."*⸮

A recent survey by the Olsten Corporation shows that the number one need of employees entering the workplace is strengthened communication skills. The survey also revealed a vast majority of companies agree that training in "people skills" yields impressive and immediate bottom line results.

You have heard people say, "How many times do I have to tell you?" Reader's Digest reported results of extended psychological studies showing:

People remember:

5 - 10% of what they hear
30 - 50% of what they hear and see
50 - 70% of what they hear, see and say
70 - 90% of what they hear, see, say, and do

So, according to the research, if all you are doing is telling them, you may have to tell them 10 to 20 times for it to sink in! This demonstrates the extraordinary value of "off your seat, on your feet" involvement.

AS SIMPLE AS 1-2-3

One of the most valuable tools that thousands of managers have gained in Turbo leadership training is this simple, basic three-step formula for helping to master a new task. Follow these three easy-to-grasp steps to provide the foundation for any instruction that is called for, either on-the-spot or in structured training sessions, with the brand-new employee or the seasoned work team who need to keep up with the latest developments in our rapidly changing workaday world.

The Six 'T's Training Model©

1. **'T'**rainer tells →→ **'T'**rainer does

2. **'T'**rainer tells → ← while **'T'**rainee does

3. **'T'**rainee tells ← ← while **'T'**rainee does

The following stories illustrate the successful use of the Six T's.

Set the Stage for Success

Sherri, customer service manager for a Portland firm, reported on a new hire's slip-up:

"It was Monday morning, bright and early on a spring day at the card lock administrator's desk. For two and a half weeks, my new hire had been doing a great job of data entry on card lock procedures. All of a sudden, I had a complaint from a customer whose order was incorrect. As a result, the customer had been overcharged. Immediately, I went into an emotional response.

I was upset and angry.

"Thankfully, I became aware of what was happening and remembered that, if I choose, I can exercise control over my response to any outside stimuli. I calmed myself down before I approached my new employee. I reminded myself that empowering leaders are not 'thermometers,' registering the atmosphere, but 'thermostats;' they control their inner climate regardless of outside circumstances.

"I dispassionately told her about the customer complaint call about the overcharge. Then I became an active listener as she began to tell me what she had done and how she had done it. To my surprise, I learned that she had misunderstood my instructions when I had trained her on this part of her job two weeks earlier. I was amazed! I had always prided myself on my training skills, but I really had blown it this time, and I told her so (Leadership Principle No. 11, *When You Blow It, Show It).*

"This was greatly appreciated by the new employee and set the tone for the training process to be conducted correctly:

→→ (Trainer **T**ells as trainer does)—I *told* her how while *showing* her how to do the data entry correctly.

→ ← (Trainer tells as **T**rainee does)—I *told* her how, step- by-step, while *she* made the data entry.

← ←(Trainee tells while **T**rainee does)—finally, I asked her to *tell me how* to do the data entry correctly as *she performed the task* a second time on her own.

"She was very happy to learn the correct procedure and told me so.

↳ *"The lesson I learned from this experience is to be very careful before I name, blame or shame others. I learned, when things go wrong, to let my first question be, 'What part did I play in this?' I also learned not to be afraid to come down to the employee's level. I could see she had greater respect for me as a person and ultimately will want to work harder to get every job done correctly the first time."*

⇄

Train for New Tasks

Marti, training coordinator for a food-service company, does an emergency save with Six T's:

"During the past few days we have hired over 100 new employees in preparation for our company's new expanded restaurant, motel and retail facilities grand opening. We found we had not prepared enough new employee orientation binders, and in what seemed like overnight, we completely depleted our supply. I did not want to start even one new hire without giving them a full and proper orientation, including the orientation three-ring binder.

"In order to stay on top of the mounds of paperwork in the Human Resources Department resulting from the rush of new employees, combined with our expanded training initiative, we recently hired a temporary utility staff person to do the various projects that none of the rest of us have time for anymore. Building these binders was a great job for her to do, so to put the task in context, I gave her a sample of the new employee orientation binder. I proceeded to explain the reason we give the binders to our new employees and some general information on the basic content. I did this to help generate more interest and insights into the project so she could take ownership of the importance of the assembling process, 'the why behind the what.'

"I then gave her a written procedure guideline to help ensure accurate binder assembly. This was just an 8-1/2 X 11 inch sheet with the steps written out. Then I carefully followed Turbo's 3-Step Show and Tell model—the Six T's. The employee followed the written outline:

→→(Trainer Tells) "I *told* her how to do the assembly as I *showed* her how to assemble a binder.

→ ←(Trainee does) "I *told* her how to properly assemble a binder as *she* put it together.

← ←(Trainee Tells) "I asked her to *tell me* the steps as Trainee does (Trainee does) *she performed* the task on her own.

"When I left her, I was very confident that she understood the importance of the project and could do the task successfully. Later, when I returned to where she was assembling the binders, I was excited to find that she had completed all 75 new employee orientation binders accurately!

↳*"The lesson I learned from this experience is that when I am specific in explaining results desired, and use the Turbo 3-step training process, team members can easily accomplish new tasks successfully."*

"Turning On" the Lathe Operator

Todd, a machine shop supervisor, learns Six T's just in time:

"Wendy was checking parts as they came off a CNC lathe. Wendy does not normally operate the CNC equipment. She seemed very eager to learn more about the machine and how to operate it.

"Although Wendy is normally a very quick learner, when she asked about how to change an offset, I shied away from giving her the training. Things were busy in the shop, and I told her I didn't have time right then to teach her how to do this somewhat advanced operation.

"I knew I was cutting Wendy short by not giving her the opportunity she deserved. We were losing a lot of her production potential. So, the following week, I approached her and offered to train her on changing the offsets at the control on the CNC lathe. She was very pleased that I was willing to take the time for her. She also liked the way I instructed her, using the easy-to-follow Six T's. Now, Wendy is able to be more independent in the shop, which helps us both.

↳*"The lesson I learned from this experience is that I must make time to train every member of my team."*

"GETTING TO KNOW"

> ⋛ *Knowledge accompanied by motivating skill is powerful.* ⋛

Is there anyone on your team who doesn't know the results expected of their team? At the heart of the quality improvement movement is an understanding that all team members gain power from continuous improvement and mastery of their job.

Expanding Opportunities

All high-performance teams are made up of empowered, knowledgeable people—people who are more than just fully trained for their own jobs—they are cross-trained so they can play more than one position. The most valuable training you can provide is, in effect, "train-the-trainer training" to help middle managers successfully provide training to their subordinates. As you give associates expanded roles and additional responsibility, you must help them acquire the abilities they need to succeed.

Top-quality organizations don't stop with just basic core competency. There is ongoing instruction in job expansion and career development, and everyone is cross-trained. Team members learn the skills needed to perform the job of the "upstream" supplier and the "downstream" customer.

Take a thorough inventory of all the tasks associates in your department must be able to perform at a high level. Make a chart like the one below, showing and numbering the tasks, the names of your associates, the task areas in which they have been trained and certified (*Cert*), and indicating training needed (*T/N*).

Team Capability Inventory

Post this chart on your department wall for all to see.

NAME	Task #1	Task #2	Task #3	Task #4	Task #4	Task #5	Task #6
Bill S	Cert	Cert	Cert	T/N	T/N	T/N	T/N
Mary B	T/N	T/N	Cert	T/N	Cert	T/N	Cert

As soon as 80% or more of your department are certified in the core competencies of your department's tasks, go on to post another similar chart and do the cross-training that is essential to expand their roles. When you have completed training your team in core competency, go on to career expansion.

↹

The "I Can Do It" Attitude

Bill, machine shop unit specialist, started with an inventory:

"In May of this year, I took inventory of the skill sets of the people on my team. It became very clear that my team members still had a lot of room for improvement. There were many skills in which they could use additional training. I decided to start with Lisa.

"My goal was to teach Lisa the steps required to set up the drill press. I carefully followed Turbo's Six T's of the Show and Tell training process.

"First, I explained each step and why I was taking it as I set up the drill press while Lisa watched me intently.

"Then I explained each step in the process to Lisa as she set up the drill press. I took my time. I know that one of my problems as a trainer in the past was going too fast.

"Now it was her turn to do it all by herself. She struggled a little and said, 'I can't do this, I'm too slow.' I replied, 'I know you can do it! In fact, I know that with a little practice, you can do it in 15 minutes or less!'

"She continued to finish the setup, and did an excellent job. Later that night, Lisa had another drill to set up. She did it herself, with no help from me. As I was doing my rounds, Lisa came up to me with an excited look on her face and said, 'I did it by myself! And I did it in 16 minutes!'

↳*"The lesson I learned from this experience is how far people will go when I show them I believe in them, give them the needed training in a way they can absorb, and tell them I know they can accomplish the new task with skill and proficiency."*

↹

TAKE THE INITIATIVE

The future depends on the competency of your team.

Your future, and the future of your company, is determined by the competency of your team. They are your future. Pay as much attention to this resource as you do your retirement account, your stock value, your 401K and your IRA.

The conclusion I have reached is that many company cultures haven't deemed training to be important enough, needed enough, or welcome in the workplace. You can change this. You can create a new company culture. Start today by giving a little training to someone on how to do one of the simpler tasks, and then another, another and still another.

Stop wasting time in meetings (another common complaint is poorly run meetings.) Use some of your meeting time for training. Make training a part of every meeting: training in basic skills for executing on the job, real training, meaningful training. Get people off their seats; role play; review the basic steps for a certain task; review the SOP; update your SOP manual. Most important of all, get people doing something!

It's easy for any of us to focus on how we're different, unique, incompatible, unlike, distinct from others around us. And yet, anytime we exercise the courage, put forth the effort, and undergo the risk of getting to know people, we almost inevitably discover we have far more in common than we realized, and that these persons are resources to us, not threats. In this story, Mitchell provides us with an example of what we can do.

↤⇥

Expanding Your Resource Pool

Mitchell, estimator and project manager, gains a "break:"

"Early in September, I broke my ankle on a project where I was working as a laborer, and was assigned light duty, working in the office. That's when I met Glen, a coworker, for the first time. Three months later, we lost one of our key estimators. The company owners offered me the position along with the training that I would need to take on the admittedly big change in my career. Though I accepted the opportunity with fear and trepidation, I was determined to give it my very best. In some ways, it represented one of the biggest challenges of my life.

"I'd been observing Glen, and how he would just come into the office and do his job without much interaction with any of the other employees, including me. I wanted to get to know Glen better. As fate would have it, in January, Glen and I were sent to Salem to deliver a bid on a project we were looking at. On our way down Interstate 5, I struck up a conversation about estimating, openly revealing my fears around my new position. I began asking Glen questions. It didn't take long before Glen opened up and started sharing with me his knowledge about estimating, and for the first time, offered to help me learn my new job. He told me he had some material in his office he wanted to give me when we got back to Portland.

"He and I swapped tales about our families and a new friendship was born. I now have a new and valuable friend, ally and resource to help me learn and perform at a higher level in my new job.

↳ *"The lesson I learned from this experience is that by taking the initiative to get to know valuable people in my world, I expand my resource pool."*

⇄

A Character Purchase

Yes, on-the-job training does take time. I refer to it as a "character purchase." Life insurance is a character purchase. You, the premium payer, never experience any direct benefit from what you pay into it. It's the beneficiary who receives the benefits.

Saving for tomorrow or for your retirement, or any other action you take today that requires effort or sacrifice with no payoff in

> ≳*If you empty your purse into your head, no one can rob you of it.*≲ —Benjamin Franklin

the present, is a character purchase. Going back to school, engaging in exercise to stay in shape, are all "character purchases."

"How-to " communication is a "character purchase" because it requires time, effort, sacrifices, maybe even direct expense, and you have no immediate benefit, payoff or advantage. It costs in time, effort, money, and courage today. You receive the benefit in the many tomorrows that follow.

SUMMARY

Actions for Empowering Leaders:

- ↻ Believe in your employees' potential
- ↻ Take time to give the needed training
- ↻ Use the Six T's of On-the-Job Training
- ↻ Give everyone the opportunity to succeed
- ↻ After core competency certification, begin cross-training

The benefits you will gain:

- ↺ You will empower everyone on the team
- ↺ You will expand the performance of your team
- ↺ You will expand your production potential
- ↺ Your employees will develop an "I-can-do-it" attitude
- ↺ You will save time and create efficiency

Conclusion

Your future success and happiness depend more on your communication ability than any other single skill. And no matter how far you rise, how successful you are, how skilled you become in communicating, there will still be room for improvement.

> You may fail to take the initiative with ↳*feedforward*/feedback.↺

> You may forget to ask for the other person's opinion, or to listen.

> You may not pay full attention to your pace, modulation and punctuation.

For me, this isn't the point. The point is the importance of your continuing pursuit of improving your communication practices. Are you trending toward improvement?

None of us is perfect, or ever will be. You never arrive at a point of perfection as a communicator. That should not discourage you, nor cause you to be complacent about improving communication, the most important of all your leadership skills.

Think of effective communication as an end result rather than an activity. Your desired end result is twofold: first, that your receiver understands your message, and second, that your receiver responds with the desired action. Strive to build understanding, support, acceptance, and committed engagement. As you do, you'll be well on your way to ensuring the success you desire for yourself, your co-workers, and your organization.

Whoever and wherever you are, whatever your role in life, the ideas in *THE LANGUAGE OF LEADERSHIP* will continue to serve you well, guiding you in eliminating communication static and improving the quality of your relationships. Empowering communication is not just about leading your team. It applies to all your interactions with everyone in your life. Your effectiveness is filtered through your communication. As long as you're in leadership at any level, your effectiveness can be improved by consistently improving your communication skills.

You have been exposed to many ideas for improving your communication skills. Now is not the time to stop. In many ways, this is a starting point, and the hope is that *THE LANGUAGE OF LEADERSHIP* leads you into a greater awareness of the importance of continuing improvement in communication.

So, above all else, the pursuit of excellence in communication is a worthwhile, never-ending, and always rewarding endeavor.

Larry W. Dennis, Sr.

ABOUT THE AUTHOR

Larry W. Dennis, Sr. is the energetic founder of Turbo Leadership Systems™. Larry has been helping businesses in the US and Canada improve their profits and performance for over thirty years.

Larry is a life-long learner who designs and implements customized leadership development programs for teams of progressive companies, leading to the improved performance and profits.

Larry is also the inventor of the patented media training system, Psycho-Actualized Learning (PAL). He is a dedicated father, and grandfather of seven who has been profiled in Secrets of Raising Teenagers Successfully. He is listed in Who's Who of the World, a member of the International Platform Association, serves on his church board, the Providence Newberg Health Foundation, and the Cascade Policy Institute board.

"Empowering your team
to ensure continuous improvement."

For more information about Larry W. Dennis, Sr and
Turbo Leadership Systems™

www.turbols.com
larry@turbols.com
cell 503-329-4519

To order books, please visit
www.turbols.com/turbo_books.html